DEFENDE

# DEFENDER OF THE FAITH

*The Church and the Crisis in the Monarchy*

Ted Harrison

**Fount**
*An Imprint of HarperCollinsPublishers*

Fount Paperbacks is an Imprint of
HarperCollins *Religious*
Part of HarperCollins *Publishers*
77–85 Fulham Palace Road, London W6 8JB

First published in Great Britain
in 1996 by Fount Paperbacks

1 3 5 7 9 10 8 6 4 2

© 1996 Ted Harrison

Ted Harrison asserts the moral right to be
identified as the author of this work

A catalogue record for this book is
available from the British Library

ISBN 0 00 627983 X

Printed and bound in Great Britain by
Caledonian International Book Manufacturing Ltd, Glasgow

# Contents

# *Acknowledgements*

In developing the ideas contained in this book I am indebted to the many dozens of people who have, over the centuries, written about the British monarchy. I have quoted, briefly or more substantially, many of them, ranging from King James I (VI) and Walter Bagehot to the royal biographers of today like Sarah Bradford and Andrew Morton. I must emphasize, however, that the conclusions I have drawn about the monarchy are entirely my own.

I have made every attempt to contact those authors who are still active and am grateful for permission to quote their words. The list of modern works on which I have drawn includes the following:

*Elizabeth*, Sarah Bradford (William Heinemann, 1996)
*Cut the Connection*, Colin Buchanan (Darton, Longman & Todd Ltd, 1994)
*Burke's Royal Families of the World: Vol. 1, Europe & Latin America* (Burke's Peerage Ltd, 1977)
*Diaries*, Alan Clark (Weidenfield & Nicolson, 1993)
*The Prince of Wales: A Biography*, Jonathan Dimbleby (Little, Brown & Co., 1994)
*The Reality of Monarchy*, Andrew Duncan (William Heinemann, 1970)
*Christian England*, David L. Edwards (3 vols., William Collins & Sons, 1981–84)

*The Tarnished Crown,* Anthony Holden (Bantam Press, 1993)
*A Church for the Nation,* Derek Jennings, edited Allen Warren (Gracewing, Fowler Wright, 1992)
*Majesty,* Robert Lacey (Sphere Books Ltd, 1978)
*The Jacobite Cause,* Bruce Lenman (Richard Drew Publishing, 1986)
*Crowned Heads,* Veronica Maclean (Hodder & Stoughton, 1994)
*Government and Parliament,* Herbert Morrison (Oxford University Press, 1954)
*Inside Kensington Palace,* Andrew Morton (Michael O'Mara Books Ltd, 1987)
*The Crowning of Elizabeth II,* L. A. Nickolls (Macdonald & Co. Ltd, 1953)
*Monarchy,* Harold Nicolson (Weidenfield and Nicolson, 1962)
*The Ultimate Family,* John Pearson (Michael Joseph Ltd, 1986)
*Royal Bounty: The Making of a Welfare Monarchy,* Frank Prochaska (Yale University Press, 1995)
*Politics in England,* Richard Rose (Faber & Faber Ltd, 1965)
*Anatomy of Britain Today,* Anthony Sampson (Hodder & Stoughton, 1965)
*The Rise & Fall of the House of Windsor,* A. N. Wilson (Reed Consumer Books Ltd, 1993)

In addition I have drawn upon a number of newspaper articles and acknowledge quotations from these in the text. I am grateful, too, to Tony Benn MP for providing me with a copy of his Bill to establish a British republic.

My thanks go as well to Giles Semper, Murray White and Thomas Allain Chapman at HarperCollins for their help and involvement during the production of this book, and special thanks to my daughter Caroline for all her help at every stage.

*Ted Harrison*
June 1996

# *Introduction*

By the unwritten Constitution of the United Kingdom of Great Britain and Northern Ireland, Her Majesty Queen Elizabeth II, as have all monarchs in recent British history, occupies the throne of her father and forebears, by the Grace of God and by the Will of the People. These are the two pillars on which the rights, privileges and duties of the Monarch rest. And it is as a direct consequence of this that the Queen's ministers derive their authority to govern in her name. Should these two pillars collapse, then the whole façade of the royal family and whole structure of the Government would, in all probability, come crashing to the ground.

Today, the House of Windsor is indeed in a perilous state. The first of the two pillars of the constitution has all but collapsed. For, as will be explored below, it becomes very difficult to sustain the notion that there is a divine authority underpinning the institution of hereditary monarchy in an increasingly secular age, when there is no longer any general or communal acceptance of the divine, or agreement as to what is meant by the word 'God'.

The survival of the second pillar, namely the Will of the People, is therefore crucial to the survival of the whole. And that rickety column can only be kept standing if the Queen and the present royal family manage to retain a general public acceptance of their position and status, however grudgingly that might be offered.

In the recent past, the royal family earned the respect of the people by representing national unity in times of danger and by being a focus of national rejoicing in times of triumph. This role has become an increasingly forlorn and irrelevant one as the country itself fragments socially and threatens to break up into constituent national units. Also, since the days of Queen Victoria, and especially during the reigns of George V and George VI, the Monarch's family has taken upon itself the role of model family and has been portrayed as upholder of all that is right, good, moral and just in society. In the early years of the Queen's reign the Windsors relied heavily on this wholesome family image, even to the extent of forbidding the marriage of one family member to a divorcé. Forty years on, critics accuse the current royal family of betrayal, hypocrisy, immorality, ineptitude, remoteness and failure in its one self-appointed task of upholding family values.

It is undeniably true that many British royal families in the past have been guilty of this and more. The debauched Hanoverians not only provided sexual and financial scandals to outrage and entertain the gossiping classes, they also brought forth a royal duke who took pleasure in massacring his father's subjects – the notorious Butcher of the Scots, the Duke of Cumberland. But that was in the days when monarchs had greater political power and at a time when the notion of a special covenant 'twixt God and the King was still current in the minds of the people. Additionally, and of equal importance, there was far less public tolerance in those days of religious diversity. There were, for instance, legal restrictions both on Roman Catholics and Jews holding public office and, amongst the many examples of the predominance in public life of the established churches, holders of a wide range of key offices were obliged to be ordained Anglicans. The God with whom the King was in covenant, was assumed, unlike today, to be an immovable and permanent part of the agreement.

What the following chapters will examine is the imminent collapse of the second pillar of the Constitution as well as the first, and the consequent forfeiture by the House of Windsor of its mandate to rule. However, this is no republican tract. Although republicanism will be examined, it will be suggested that in many respects it is a far from adequate alternative to the *status quo*.

Anthony Holden's book about the royal family, *The Tarnished Crown*, closes with these words:

> With a Monarch-in-waiting apparently unsure of his own future, this has to be the hour for his potential subjects to consider theirs. Britain is long overdue a profound and vigorous reappraisal of its constitution. Whatever the resulting reforms, and whenever they are implemented...it is a debate which must begin in earnest now.

This book is an early salvo in that debate. It takes the whole matter far further than the hitherto accepted limits to that debate – the simple idea that the only alternative to a monarchy is an elected president. It will explore a much wider range of options as to how the House of Windsor can be peaceably replaced, leaving the British Constitution unharmed, and in all probability enhanced and improved. The time is certainly right for this change, as all the institutions of Government, including Parliament, which derive their authority in turn from the Queen, are ripe for reform.

There are three additional factors pressing for an urgent restructure of the Constitution which must inevitably raise new questions about the continuation on the throne of the present Monarch. One is the possible break up of the United Kingdom. Will an independent Scotland ask the Queen to remain on the throne? Another involves the search for a lasting peace in Northern Ireland. If the monarchy, in its present form, were removed from the equation, would it be easier to find a long-term political solution in the province? And the third factor is this – the growing separation from Britain of the old Commonwealth, following the loss of the British empire. There is already a strong tide flowing in the direction of republicanism in Australia, the notion is gaining favour in New Zealand, and one day Quebec might decide to become separated from Canada and wish to discard the Crown. Can these Commonwealth reforms be most effectively accomplished as part and parcel of the entire reform of the monarchy?

It can be argued that the present monarchy only survives because the British people have no stomach for republicanism. They do not want to see the Queen replaced by a party politician as president. This is probably true, but why should the established order remain unreformed because the search for a viable alternative has been too restricted? It is a time for imaginative lateral thinking. It could be possible to retain the monarchy and replace the House of Windsor. Or, it might be possible to maintain the Crown but remove from the Crown an hereditary family whose only role in life is to provide a member to wear it.

In exploring all the other options, one key lesson of British history should be borne in mind. The unwritten Constitution of these islands is a very flexible beast. It can metamorphose in any way the nation chooses to meet the requirements of the age. And in this context it should not be forgotten that, at various times in history, royal houses have fallen out of favour or failed to provide a suitable heir from amongst the Monarch's immediate family. At such times one royal dynasty can give way to another.

Since 1066, when the Norman dynasty defeated King Harold II and superseded (or usurped) the Saxon line, eleven families or royal houses have occupied the English throne or seat of government: the House of Normandy, the House of Anjou (The Plantagenets), the House of Lancaster, the House of York, the House of Tudor, the House of Stuart, the Protectorate of Oliver and his son Richard Cromwell, the House of Orange, the House of Hanover, the House of Saxe-Coburg and Gotha, and the House of Windsor. The average life span of a dynasty has been 84.5 years. By the start of the new millennium in AD 2001, the House of Windsor, declared and named by King George V during the First World War, will have been custodians of the British Crown for 84 years. Its time is nearly up.

# 1

# *By Divine Right?*

The modern British twenty-pence piece is a mediocre, utilitarian little coin. It is seven sided with smoothed corners and only 22 millimetres in diameter. It was introduced into the pockets and purses of the British public as one of the new generation of decimal coins following the abolition of the old system of money when twenty shillings were worth a pound and there were twelve pennies in every shilling.

To look at, the coin resembles a metal nut. There is no evidence that it has found its way into the affections of the British people. It is now a piece of disposable small change which in its own right can seldom even buy a cup of tea.

On the reverse, in an undistinguished font, the words 'TWENTY PENCE' are written. The figure '20' is also given, as well as a date, and there is a basic and unmemorable floral design surmounted by a crown. Turn the coin over, and there is a portrait of the Queen, a stiff, formal and barely recognizable profile. Around a raised rim is the inscription 'ELIZABETH II' and seven curious capital letters: 'D.G.REG.F.D.'.

When decimal coinage was introduced, out went a system of coinage familiar since medieval times. Discarded also were some beautifully designed coins bearing such romantic nicknames as florin, half crown, bob and tanner. All that has now survived of the old media of exchange are those seven strange capital letters.

They have been preserved on all modern British coins for they represent the very authority of the monarchy. They are the distillation of the mysterious link which is believed to exist between the Monarch and God. Therefore, as in Britain all power – legislative, executive and judicial – stems from the Monarch, those seven letters, representing five words of Latin, give legitimacy to all branches of the British government.

The first two letters, 'D.G.', are the initial letters of the Latin *Dei Gratia*, translated as 'By the Grace of God'; the central three letters are an abbreviation for *Regina*, the Latin for Queen; and the final two, 'F.D.', represent the Latin words *Fidei Defensor*, meaning 'Defender of the Faith'.

Elizabeth II, as Queen of the United Kingdom of Great Britain and Northern Ireland, is at the centre of everything in British public life. All constitutional and legal routes and powers lead back to her. Members of the police, Parliament, the law courts, the armed forces, the established churches and many, many other branches owe direct allegiance to one woman. Governments can do almost anything by invoking her name. For instance, the preamble to the highly controversial Security Service Bill laid before Parliament shortly before Christmas in 1995, designed to extend the powers of MI5, begins with the standard formula of words, 'Be it enacted by the Queen's most Excellent Majesty...'.

Her direct powers have been whittled down over the centuries, but her symbolic importance has not. She, in turn, is descended from monarchs who in the past wielded almost absolute power and claimed they ruled by divine right. While this notion may have lain dormant for many centuries, there has been no dilution of the claim, vigorously declaimed at the coronation in 1953, that the British nation, through the mediation of the Queen, is a nation under God, whose very institutions have a divine seal of approval. To make sure of this authority and to make it known to everyone in the land who cares to remind themselves, even the meanest of coins carries the inscription that the Monarch, of whom all British people are subjects, is Queen by the Grace of God and Defender of the Faith.

Thus it is that when the future of the monarchy in Britain is examined, more is at stake than the future twists in the real-life soap opera of the Windsor family. What is at stake is the future understanding by the British people of themselves as part of history, part of a Christian heritage, subscribers to a mystical pact with the Almighty through their sovereign leader. With a replacement of the monarchy by a presidency, is there a real danger of the whole fiction of Britain – the nation state, collapsing? Might the self-image and self-esteem of over 50 million people implode with it?

The existence of such fears perhaps explains why republicanism is not, and has seldom, if ever, been an option favoured by the British. Even today, with the Windsor family in disarray, polls like the Granada MORI survey show only 23 per cent of the British people in favour of abolishing the monarchy. Republicanism is too fundamental a change in identity, as will be explored later, and too unsettling a notion to contemplate. Who knows what social chaos or disintegration might follow such a revolution?

Yet, many would argue that Britain cannot continue for ever in a state of self-delusion. The fairy-tale of Britain and its special relationship with God through the Sovereign has been at the heart of much injustice and inequality, even brutality, both at home and around the world. It gave the British a false sense of importance which justified them annexing much of the globe in the nineteenth century in the name of Queen, country and Empire. Today, it enables police to don riot gear and help Governments and road builders smash their way through people's homes. Claiming to be maintaining the Queen's peace, the police arrest and bully those who object. A whole edifice of privilege is maintained through the monarchy and the gifts which are distributed by the Queen and her government in her name. Furthermore it is illegal even to contemplate the Queen's demise under the Treason and Felony Act.

Nevertheless the British fairy-tale is a powerful myth. For many years it was unquestioned. An acquiescent and docile people, say the radicals, revered the Monarch, cheered the flag, stood to attention for the national anthem and never, like the French, dared to take to rioting in the streets. And that reverence for the Queen took, and still within many Establishment circles takes, a peculiar form. She is viewed with an awe which attaches uniquely to herself and which is incomprehensible to any foreigner who has not shared in the British culture from birth. Even the most hardened captains of industry go weak-kneed and weak-minded at the thought of shaking hands with the Queen, let alone welcoming her to their factory or going to Buckingham Palace to receive a knighthood. The British people accept rules of protocol which are absurd and which go totally unquestioned when the Queen or one of her near family is involved. Women must curtsey in a prescribed manner; the royal hand if proffered must be shaken in a certain way; there are rules to be followed in having conversations. Even to initiate a conversation with a member of the royal family is considered bad manners and a breach of protocol and etiquette. No wonder that when a former Australian Prime Minister put a gentle arm on the Queen's back to guide her in the right direction, the British Establishment was scandalized!

Yet, paradoxically, the British people also love to read the gossip about the royals. They have strong opinions about the state of the royal marriages. Many of the older generation will know as much about the family details of the Windsors as they know about their own families. There is a tradition, too, going back many centuries, of mocking the royal family, laughing at their foibles, disapproving of their antics.

This however should not be mistaken for disrespect although it is certainly a paradox. This apparent contradiction can best be understood within the context of a sense of religious awe.

There is a similar tradition one could say of the British people mocking and laughing at the Church. The caricature vicar is an instantly recognizable character in popular comedy. Bishops are frequently figures of fun. Yet when people – especially those who have only infrequent contacts with the Church – enter a hallowed building at a time of celebration or need, a wedding or a funeral, the scoffing and the joking is largely left outside. Perhaps it is the unfamiliarity of the surroundings, the formality of the setting, the important event being celebrated, which is brought to bear on them, but a sense of awe and insecurity descends. People look at each other anxiously for some signal as to when to stand and when to kneel. People want to be sure they are wearing the right clothes for the occasion and no one has left on a hat which should have been taken off. It may be that on such occasions people find themselves in the presence of God and therefore behave in this way; or it could be said that they find themselves in touch, in some awesome way with the roots of their very identity.

It is something very similar to this which happens when ordinary British people have fleeting contact with the Sovereign. However much an individual might have tut-tutted at Fergie or made jokes about the Queen's corgis, in her presence, or in that of any member of her family, the same nervousness, awe and insecurity descends.

Thus it is that to understand the role of the Monarch in society one has to understand the role of the Monarch within the context of national identity and the nation's relationship with and understanding of God.

For a new nation like Australia to discard the monarchy might seem a relatively simple process. For an old nation like Britain, it is not simply a matter of replacing a weary, discredited and privileged family with a figurehead or president. It is a matter of deconstructing a nation's identity and relationship with God.

It could well be argued that it is a process that has begun to happen the other way round, and that the nation is losing its identity because the monarchy is at present de-constructing itself. But it is not that simple. One process feeds off the other. The nation has lost its coherent sense of spiritual purpose and so the monarchy is in decline, and as the monarchy declines so the nation loses its spiritual cohesion even further.

If the process of de-construction is allowed to continue, what might the result be? In the immediate future there seems very little likelihood of a presidential system being inaugurated, but many other radical changes might take place. The Church of England could sever its links with the Crown and become one of a number of British Christian denominations. This would result in English people ceasing to be members of that church solely by living in the country and having access to its parish structure. A similar severance of the Church of Scotland's links with the Monarch could also arguably weaken the parish structure north of the border. The established churches would then demand of worshippers an adherence to dogma and creeds and evidence of true commitment. Couples wishing to marry in church would have to sign up as members weeks in advance and prove their Christian credentials. It would be a move welcomed by many Christian enthusiasts, but it would be the death of the nation's folk faith. The unchurched would be left in an alarming spiritual vacuum.

And what might fill that vacuum? A re-dedication to materialism and the consumer society? Political extremism? A turning to the pantheon of New Age ideas and the attempt being made by many to recreate the mystery and magic of a supposed pre-industrial golden age? Events might take any number of unpredictable turns. There might even be a curious reaction to the process with a new contract between the Crown and God being devised. This will be examined in more detail in the later chapter on the future of the Princess of Wales, the one and only member of the royal family with the charisma to revitalize the spiritual link. If she does, however, that new bond between God, Crown and people will be very different from that of old. It will undoubtedly be of and for a new age.

The mystical, almost magical link between Monarch and God can be traced, Sir Harold Nicolson argued, back to pre-industrial cultures. Its roots lie in the Shaman of hunter gatherer tribes. They were both healers and priests who through ritual and by virtue of descent and inherited powers communed with the gods and provided physical and psychological healing to the community. These Shamans, or medicine men came from a caste or oligarchy and had the secrets transmitted to them through the family. As society became more urbanized, the Shaman became the sorcerer kings. 'The rise of monarchy,' Nicolson observed, 'appears to be the essential condition of the emergence of mankind from savagery.' During various stages of evolution, monarchs have become gods, warriors, philosophers as well as healers.

The British monarchy over the centuries has contained something of all these elements, stopping short, perhaps, of laying claim to divine status. Even though the lone republican back in the sixties and seventies, the Labour MP Willie Hamilton, once caustically observed in the days when the royals were still in favour, 'as a nation we have forsaken God for Elizabeth II with Prince Philip as a latter-day John the Baptist', no British monarch has ever claimed to be a god-like figure. Unlike the Emperor of Japan or the Roman Caesars, British monarchs have never been that presumptuous – although the Stuarts came very close!

The powers of healing, however, have been claimed. Even 300 years ago, the touch of the King was said to heal a number of conditions. The royal touch, it was said, was particularly appropriate to scrofula patients and the practice it is said began with Edward the Confessor, King and Saint. Queen Anne, as late as 1712, continued the practice, and Samuel Johnson recalls how he was taken to her as a little boy to be healed. The practice did not die out entirely until the nineteenth century when Cardinal York, Bonnie Prince Charlie's younger brother and the Jacobite pretender, performed the rite in Rome in 1807. In addition to the royal touch there were the cramp-rings which, having been touched by the Monarch, were handed out as cures for a variety of conditions. In Mary Tudor's time, it was prayed that those who received them 'may be preserved from the wiles of Satan, spasms of the nerves and the perils of the epilepsy'. She would pray that the rings be sanctified, 'even as God had sanctified her hands with his holy oil'.

Little over a generation ago, the ancient relationship between God and the Monarch was believed to be timeless. If it changed and evolved it was only very slowly. However, in the same way that there have been huge changes in society, science, medicine, communications and the arts, the last 40 years have seen equally major changes in the way in which the monarchy is perceived. Some mystery remains in the public mind, as does much awe and the accompanying deference, but nothing like that which existed at the time of the accession and the coronation of Queen Elizabeth II. Looking at the flickering grey pictures and listening to the hushed reverential tones of Richard Dimbleby, the old recordings of the coronation service of 1953 are unmistakably from a former age. Who could have thought then that within the time span of the Queen's reign the sacred rite would be considered unrepeatable. For that carefully choreographed mystery of the coronation, which provided legitimacy for the government and stability for a unified nation, contains so much which would appear laughable today that it would need to be totally rewritten.

In the words of Church of England Synod Member Bishop Colin Buchanan,

The Archbishop of Canterbury must be praying fervently for the Queen's health every day. For if she died tomorrow I wouldn't want to be in his shoes recommending to the King Charles how he should be crowned.

The question of Diana's appearance at the service, or perhaps more poignantly her absence, would be but a side show to the other problems presented by such an occasion.

Looking back at the early years of Queen Elizabeth II's reign, many younger people must be amazed at the fawning adoration of that coronation day which bordered on superstition. John Pearson, in his 1986 book *The Ultimate Family*, took a look back to those quaint old days. Such was the hope abroad in the country for a new start, a new great Elizabethan era, that, as Pearson put it, people were expecting the Queen to work miracles. Belief in the miraculous nature of kingship is extremely ancient, but had all but vanished in Britain after good Queen Anne had dutifully 'touched' her afflicted subjects as a cure for scrofula. But, thanks to Richard Dimbleby and the widespread sense of personal involvement with the Queen at the moment of her crowning, television audiences could now experience that authentic sense of 'the sacredness of the royal person' with which Queen Mary, Queen Elizabeth II's grandmother, had habitually approached her husband.

The Queen, however, over her 44-year reign, has never been a miracle worker or ever had the inclination or charisma to pretend to be. But does she believe in miracles? Is she a woman of deep spirituality, a poser of profound questions, a pilgrim on a journey of religious exploration?

Her own personal faith, as far as it can be discerned, is typical of that embraced by many in the upper classes. Church-going is a duty, and a public one at that. Deep theology is of little interest but a rousing sermon much enjoyed for its stimulation. Clues emerge as to her true spiritual code from her Christmas Day homilies, where she makes worthy exhortations to the Commonwealth, praises good work and example, and invites God's blessing on her subjects. Her 1991 Christmas message was made at a time when she must have been aware that the Windsor family life was crumbling around her. She took the moment to affirm her continuing determination to go on serving the nation according to her sacred charge after 40 years on the throne. Her words, however, were misunderstood by a number of observers who thought they detected in her address not a reaffirmation of her idea of her divine duty but a put-down to Prince Charles. They heard her giving a public signal that she did not intend to abdicate in his favour. 'With your prayers and your help, and the love and support of my family, I shall try and help you in the years to come.'

In his biography of the Prince of Wales, Jonathan Dimbleby describes the Queen's faith as 'unambiguously in the tradition of her Anglican inheritance'. That is, of course, except when she is in Scotland, as Andrew Duncan pointed out rather neatly in his book *The Reality of Monarchy*. 'The Queen's relationship to God changes as she moves over the Scottish border. She becomes less important.' Not to God one presumes, but as a figure on the religious landscape.

In England, the custom of bishops being appointed by the Monarch developed from the dark ages, and was made statute law during the Reformation in the sixteenth century. Henry VIII deprived the Pope of any residual powers to appoint to English Sees and had himself declared 'the only supreme head in earth of the Church of England'. Elizabeth I more modestly altered 'head' to 'Governor', and that is the position of Queen Elizabeth II today. In Scotland, she upholds the Presbyterian faith of the established Church of Scotland, as she promised at her coronation, but never suggest to a minister that she is Head of the Kirk or a very sharp correction will follow.

Nevertheless, both north and south of the border, the Queen makes frequent references to the Almighty. Yet it has to be asked to what extent her public utterances include references to the divine because she has a deep trust in God and the power of prayer, and to what extent they are part of the historic formula of the British monarchy. It is hard to ascertain. When she calls on God to bless a ship or the deliberations of Parliament, she is more likely to be taking part in the ritual of office. When she speaks to her clergy, one might suppose her words of encouragement come less from the conscience and heart than well-rehearsed formulae.

In 1969, the Queen addressed the General Assembly of the Church of Scotland thus:

Christians everywhere are sustained and inspired by the ideal of the brotherhood of man and the commandment to love one another. In this imperfect world the struggle to achieve this ideal is long and hard but we all look to the leadership of the Church and we are most conscious of its unceasing efforts. There may be an inclination to look back at the apparent lack of progress but it is far better to look forward with hope, with faith and with expectation.

The world may often seem gloomy and discouraging but we should remember that we are only able to witness a very small part of its continuing development; we should remember that with courage and perseverance we can do God's will in the certain knowledge that he expects us to fulfil his grand design.

In this there is work for the most humble. Injustice, suffering and ignorance cry out for remedy all around us. Church people have every opportunity to set an example of service and self-sacrifice so as to make this world a better place for all people.

All good, worthy sentiments, but she gave nothing away as to her own personal spirituality or faith. Was she mindful of her duties to her other subjects and to those in the Commonwealth, believing she should not appear to say anything in public which might offend those of different faiths? For nothing in the above quote was so specifically Christian that it could not have been endorsed by a devout Muslim, Jew or Hindu.

For much of the history of Britain these multi-faith considerations were irrelevant. What was more important to a monarch choosing his or her words was that through medieval times and beyond, the Church and State have lived in tension. The Church in England, under the supreme governorship of the Bishop of Rome, the Pope, maintained an independence from the State. The Monarch, lord of every subject through the feudal hierarchy, was answerable only to God.

John Wycliff, the fourteenth-century theologian and translator of the Bible, wrote a pamphlet justifying the divine right of kings in this way. He said that God favoured kingship since three kings had been designated to visit the manger at Bethlehem. And he went on to claim, to quote Nicolson's summary:

> The king must be honoured as the vicar of God *(rex enim est Dei vicarius)* and our awe of the king is a reflection of our fear of God. The king possesses 'palpable' *(sensibilis)* dignity, whereas the dignity of the Church is impalpable. Thus even a bad king should be revered owing to the office and titles that he holds. The priest should own no possessions or titles, since Christ himself was poor.

The Church – prior to Reformation, the Roman Catholic Church – was accepted by everyone including the Monarch to be God's representative on earth. The King was therefore the vassal of the Church and yet Sovereign, within the boundaries of his kingdom, of all its members individually. From time to time, the tension exploded into violence, the martyrdom of Thomas Becket of Canterbury being the best known occasion.

The situation changed in the sixteenth century under Henry VIII for two reasons. Firstly, the ideas of the Reformation were sweeping through Europe, and a Church which was seen by many to be corrupt was under threat. People were beginning to feel that they too should have direct access to the Scriptures, and ideas were forming about the individual's responsibility to God which bypassed the Church as intermediary. At the same time in England there were special circumstances pertaining to the King. He was a ruthless and ambitious man who dismissed the Church of Rome's claims to spiritual jurisdiction in his kingdom by himself becoming the Church of England's supreme head. The issue which triggered this is well known – his desire to be divorced from his first wife.

It is an irony that Henry VIII embarked on his break with Rome only four years after he had been awarded the title

'Defender of the Faith' by Pope Leo X for his defence of the sacraments against Martin Luther. David Edwards, in *Christian England*, summarized the final break in this way: 'Henry summoned the "Reformation Parliament" which enacted nothing less than a revolution...exalting the Crown above the Church as it had never been exalted before.' Edwards continued:

> All payment to, and legal business in, Rome were forbidden, and it was no longer heresy to deny the pope's primacy. The king alone was to appoint bishops and was to receive a tenth of all clerical incomes. The earlier submission of the clergy to the king as their 'Supreme Head' was turned into English law without any reference to the saving clause about the 'law of Christ'. It was made treason even to speak (let alone act) against the king as a 'heretic, schismatic, tyrant, infidel, or usurper of the crown'. The Preamble to the Statute of Appeals in 1533 declared that, on the contrary, 'by divers sundry old authentic histories and chronicles it is manifestly declared ...that this realm of England is an empire...governed by one supreme head and king...unto whom a body politic, compact of all sort and degrees of people, divided in terms and by names of spirituality and temporality, be bounded and owe to bear next to God a natural and humble obedience...'

The King succeeded through this drastic step in divorcing his wife and indeed went on to have five other wives, but he never attempted to restore the old status of the church once his primary object was achieved. As David Edwards put it, 'He liked being the English Church's 'Supreme Head'; it suited his consummate vanity.'

It would appear that many of his reigning descendants have felt the same. Although in Henry's case there was one other convincing reason for him to remain in charge of the Church. He had his eye on Church property and the wealth of the monasteries, and in due course set about ruthlessly to abolish the religious communities and expropriate their entire wealth.

The seventeenth century saw politics and faith entirely intertwined in a brutal period which culminated in the Civil War. However, the legacy of the century has not been entirely negative, for it was King James I who authorized the publication of the new translation of the Bible, a translation which brought new beauty to the Scriptures and to the English language. It made the Bible accessible to the people, and has survived and is much-cherished to this day.

It was King James I, of England and the VI of Scotland, who set out in unequivocal form the view of the Monarch as God's representative on earth. Having shed the intermediary of the Pope, it was possible for him to lay claim to a hierarchical view of society which placed God at the head of the spiritual order, but monarchs firmly, with divine permission, at the head of all earthly order.

In his speech to the Lords and Commons of the Parliament in 1610, he declared, 'the state of monarchy is the supremest thing upon earth. For Kings are not only God's lieutenants upon earth, and sit upon God's throne but even by God Himself they are called gods.' Later in the same address he justified his views by saying that kings are called gods, for

...they exercise a manner or resemblance of divine power upon earth. For if you will consider the attributes to God, you shall see how they agree in the person of a King. God has power to create, or destroy, make, or unmake at His pleasure, to give life, or send death, to judge all, and to be judged nor accountable to none; to raise low things, and to make high things low at his pleasure, and to God are both soul and body due. And the like power have kings: they make and unmake their subjects; they have power of raising and casting down, of life and of death; judges over all their subjects, and in all cases, and yet accountable to none but God only. They have power to exalt low things and abase high things, and make of their subjects like men at the chess:

a pawn to take a bishop or a knight, and to cry up or down any of their subjects, as they do their money. And to the king is due both the affection of the soul and the service of the body of his subjects...

This extravagant justification of his status, while accepted by many of his listeners, did not go unchallenged, and over the next fifty years the notion of the King as God's lieutenant on earth was at the heart of one of Britain's most bloody internal disputes.

It was King James's son Charles who came to the throne in 1625, who bore the brunt of the physical challenge to what he perceived as his divinely ordained position. He died on the scaffold 24 years later, viewed by many as an English martyr to this cause.

The conflict and disputes of the Civil War can be seen as a secular struggle for power between a monarchy and an aristocracy on the one hand and the emerging professional middle class on the other. However, all the rhetoric of the debate was couched in religious terminology. King Charles insisted that his political position was bolstered by his divine right to rule. At every stage, on the other hand, the Parliamentarians invoked the Almighty and indeed could only contemplate the extreme step of regicide by believing that they were morally and divinely justified. In the end, the King was tried for treason, with the implication that he had acted contrary to the best interests both of his people and of God.

On the scaffold, the King approached death with a much noted dignity. The crowd did not cheer but groaned as his severed head was held aloft. Prayers and meditations attributed to the King were published and in the long run a valuable mystique was added to the monarchy by his execution.

It is difficult to disentangle the claims of the Stuart monarchs to rule by divine right and their political interests. It was very useful for the Stuarts in their political power struggle with the God-fearing puritans to claim such a divine link. In the British context, too, it has enabled the Monarch to legitimize the way in which on matters ecclesiastical the Pope was bypassed in Britain. After the Restoration in 1681, the doctrine of divine right was still maintained and expressed in this way in an address approved by the University of Cambridge and presented to Charles II.

> We still believe and maintain that our Kings derive not their title from the people but from God; to Him only they are accountable; that it belongs not to subjects either to create or censor, but to honour and obey their sovereign, who comes to be so by a fundamental hereditary right of succession, which no religion, no law, no fault or forfeiture can alter or diminish.

It was following the restoration of Charles I's son Charles II to the throne that the position of the Church of England within the structure of the nation was formalized in an Act of Uniformity. Once royal assent was granted in 1661, 'every parson, vicar or other minister whatsoever' had to declare his 'unfeigned assent and consent to all and everything contained and prescribed' in the new edition of the Book of Common Prayer. It also had to be declared by ministers of the Church that they acknowledged as unlawful 'upon any pretence whatsoever, to take arms against the king'.

The Book of Common Prayer remained for over three centuries at the heart of the Church of England. Only with the introduction of Alternative Services in recent times has it been superseded. While other provinces of the Anglican communion world-wide experimented with government and liturgy, the Church of England remained legally committed to the old formularies.

To take an old Prayer Book of just a century ago is to travel in one's mind, as if in a time capsule, to an age where the total absorption of Monarch and Church within each other was entirely proper and acceptable. The deference shown by the Church to the Monarch, indeed suggested that little had died of the notion of the divine right of kings on the scaffold with King Charles.

The Victorian Prayer Book continued to give forms of prayer for thanksgiving on the day of the accession of the Monarch. It was described as a solemn day for which a particular service was appointed. The Collect began: 'Most gracious God, who hast set thy servant VICTORIA, our Queen, upon the Throne of her Ancestors', and continues later, 'do thou weaken the hands, blast the designs and defeat the enterprises of all her enemies, that no secret conspiracies, nor open violences, may disquiet her Reign'.

And another prayer yields 'unfeigned thanks, for that thou wast pleased, as on this day, to place Thy Servant our Sovereign Lady, Queen VICTORIA upon the Throne of this Realm'.

In addition, a prayer for the Royal Family is included at both Morning and Evening Prayer, the two offices said or sung until comparatively recently in church every Sunday and in cathedrals every day.

Almighty God, the fountain of all goodness, we humbly beseech thee to bless Albert Edward Prince of Wales, the Princess of Wales, and all the Royal Family: Endue them with thy Holy Spirit; enrich them with thy heavenly grace; prosper them with all happiness; and bring them to thine everlasting kingdom: through Jesus Christ our Lord.

Furthermore, in the Communion service, immediately before the reading of the Epistle, a form of prayer was set out for the Queen as 'supreme Governor of this Church'. It began, 'Blessed Lord who hast called Christian Princes to the defence of thy Faith, and hast made it their duty to promote the spiritual welfare, together with the temporal interest of their people ...'

The penultimate section of the Book of Common Prayer, placed just before the tables laying out whom a man and a woman may not marry, consists of the Thirty-Nine Articles of

Religion. These date from before the Act of Uniformity to the reign of Queen Elizabeth, when, in 1571, the articles were drawn up and then subscribed to by the bishops of the Church. Traditionally, the articles lay out what is distinct in theology and practice about the Church of England, and the clergy have been expected to assent to them in a public declaration.

In Article Thirty-Seven, 'the Queen's Majesty' is acknowledged to have the chief power in the Realm, 'whether they be ecclesiastical or civil'. Later, the thirty-seventh article talks of the prerogative of all Godly princes to 'rule all estates and degrees committed to their charge by God, whether they be Ecclesiastical or Temporal, and restrain with the civil sword the stubborn and evil-doers'.

Certain sections of the Book of Common Prayer have been removed in later times. The prayers prescribed as thanksgiving for the thwarting of the gun-powder plot have been disposed of, for example. Nevertheless thousands of older Anglicans will be very familiar with these words from the Prayer Book:

ALMIGHTY God, Whose kingdom is everlasting, and power infinite; Have mercy upon the whole Church; and so rule the heart of Thy chosen servant ELIZABETH our Queen and Governor, that she (knowing whose minister she is) may above all things seek Thy honour and glory: and that we, and all her subjects (duly considering whose authority she hath), may faithfully serve, honour and humbly obey her...

The overall sentiment therefore of the surviving Prayer Book is still not much altered from that of the 1660s. What has happened of late, however, is that the Book of Common Prayer has fallen into disuse. Today, the Alternative Service Book (1980) tones down much of the royalist content. At Morning Prayer there is a brief response referring to the Monarch: 'O Lord save the Queen; and teach her counsellors wisdom.' In the Litany, God is asked to guard and strengthen his servant the Queen, 'that she may put her trust in you and seek your honour and glory'.

There are three State Prayers which the ASB sets out for optional use. The first asks for God's blessing on the Queen and those in authority under her. A similar blessing is asked for the royal family, with an emphasis on an enrichment of their personal faith, while the third of the prayers refers to the structures of the Church.

If there were ever a move in Britain towards republicanism or other radical change to the position of the Queen, any reprint of the Alternative Service Book would contain just a few marginal amendments.

Indeed, today, most members of the Church of England going to a family Eucharist or morning service on a Sunday can go from one year to the next without ever offering a formal prayer to God on behalf of the Queen. The Church has not been disestablished, but, for most practical purposes, the Queen and the royal family have been marginalized in the life of the Church of England.

These changes in the Church feed the process of what Bishop Colin Buchanan calls 'a dedivinization' of the monarchy. Was it a gradual realization that this process was eroding a keystone of the institution that, within the last year, caused Buckingham Palace to make moves to re-establish its position? The most significant decision was the appointment of the Princess Royal as the Queen's High Commissioner to the Church of Scotland General Assembly in May 1996. This office north of the border is the remnant of a tussle between Church and Monarch every bit as passionate north of the border as south.

During the reigns of James VI and Charles I, the central theme of Scottish history was the Royal attempt to increase arbitrary power and the national resistance to this which was led by the Church.

The main bones of contention were matters of ritual and of Episcopal government, with the Crown trying to impose its views and to govern the Church and influence Parliament through a subservient hierarchy. The right to summon General Assemblies of the Church of Scotland was also an important point and here King James succeeded in exerting his authority. It was enacted in 1584 that no Assembly should be held without his command. When an Act of Parliament of 1592 established a full Presbyterian system, it was laid down that the King, or his Commissioner, if present before the dissolving of the Assembly, should appoint the time and place for the next Assembly. This power was often used both to defer Assemblies and to change their meeting places. King James was present himself at about nine different Assemblies, and sometimes spoke and voted. Otherwise, he was usually represented by one or more officials or members of the Privy Council. It is pointed out by the present Purse Bearer, the Chamberlain to the Queen's High Commissioner, that the last Royal appearance was in 1602, and that no Sovereign attended the General Assembly in person thereafter until October 1960, when the Queen attended a Special Session of the Assembly to mark the 400th Anniversary of the Celebration of the Reformation.

As we come to the end of the twentieth century and of the second millennium, much has changed. Political passions in many areas run high, but the battlegrounds of old have been largely forgotten. Britain is a multi-faith society, with Muslims being the second most numerous group after Christians. Church membership and attendance is in steady decline. At the time of the Queen's accession, 65 per cent of all children born in England were baptized. Today the figure is 25 per cent. Similarly in the early 1950s, 6.5 per cent of all people over 15 years of age took Holy Communion at Easter. Today, the figure has fallen below 4 per cent. In Scotland, there is a similar tale to tell. At the start of the present queen's reign, 1.25 million Scots were members of the established church. Since then that figure has fallen by over half a million to 720,000, and by the year 2005 the projected membership will be down to 500,000.

Within the established churches there have been huge changes. Not only has the Anglican rite of Holy Communion as used at the coronation service only 43 years ago been largely superseded, there has been a major theological shift away from the safe Anglican centre ground. Theologically, it would be no exaggeration to say that the middle ground has all but evaporated. Liberal theologians (who would give short shrift to the mumbo-jumbo of the coronation ritual) form one powerful group, and most numerous in opposition to them are the charismatic evangelicals who are far more concerned about revival and renewal than they are in any old-fashioned religious claims that the Queen's supporters might make about her. Indeed, most new Christians of the current wave of charismatic enthusiasm would see these aspects of old Anglicanism as being at the very heart of what was wrong with the old church. They want to get back to the simplicities of the early Christians, before the princes of the church began to compromise the Gospel with the world of politics and power.

The Queen and her advisers must now surely realize that to claim to reign by the Grace of God is a nonsense in a secular society. And, in addition to having no credibility with non-believers, such notions have also earned the indifference of the regular members of the established churches. This must be especially damning to the traditional monarchy. From the point of view of worshipping members of the established churches, there would be no special theological upheaval involved if the nation was to switch from being a monarchy to some other form of government. Indeed, as will be suggested later when the more specific consequences of disestablishment are explored, it could well be argued that church members are already well down the road towards complete separation of their secular and religious lives, and that the Monarch has no place in the latter.

It should be pointed out here that a decline in membership of the established churches does not however imply that all churches are suffering a fall in attendance. Certainly the main free churches are struggling, and the Roman Catholics have seen a fall off in regular attendance at Mass, but it does not follow that an interest in matters spiritual is on the wane. A number of unofficial, fringe Christian churches have seen spectacular growth.

A broader perspective on the changes which have taken place which have impinged so radically on society's understanding of the religious role of the Monarch comes from an address given by the historian Karen Armstrong in January 1996. What she observed was a general change in the way God was perceived by Western Christians.

> Many of our ideas about God are dying, but new ones will arise. The idea of God has changed constantly through the ages. Every age has to make their own image of God. Often the idea of God has changed very dramatically indeed.

Given this approach, it is easy to argue that the image of God held by almost everyone in society has changed since the Queen's coronation. The God invoked by the aristocratic Anglican majesty of the Abbey service is unrecognizable to the modern ASB Anglicans, charismatic fundamentalists, let alone the members of the numerous pseudo-Christian cults and of the ever-growing pantheistic New Age movement.

Consequently, bit by bit, the Sovereign is losing her spiritual justification to remain in her position of privilege at the head of the nation. For the sovereign would appear to be one of the very few people left whose image of God has not changed with the times. Soon, except on a few occasions such as a royal wedding or a Remembrance Day service, any surviving spiritual role for the Monarch will be entirely lost. Already, the Cenotaph rituals are losing their *raison d'être* as the war generation dies. That connection between Church, Monarch and war is meaningless to almost everyone but the elderly. The troops of the First World War might have rallied to King and country and believed that God was on their side, but very few of them now remain. Those who fought in the Second World War were motivated somewhat differently. The idea that British troops would fight for King and country unquestioningly had faded away on the battlefields of the Somme. Those who fought in the Second World War were far more directly motivated to fight to save their own families and homes from an obvious and brutal ideology. As for royal weddings – will the Windsor family ever again have the bare-faced cheek to stage a fairy-tale wedding, after four of the most recent have ended in divorce or separation? No wonder Prince Edward and his long-term partner appeared reluctant to 'name the day'.

There will be those who will argue, and in all probability they will include the Queen herself, that it is quite improper and illogical to advocate the case that a Monarch no longer rules by the Grace of God simply because his or her people cease to believe in God. God exists, they will say, whether people believe in him or not.

If God does not exist, then the Monarch rules solely by the Will of the People, and if the willingness of the people to support the Monarch is diminished because they no longer believe in God, then so be it. But that is a very different argument from maintaining that the living God's authority granted to the Monarch has been withdrawn because the people no longer believe in his reality.

This approach raises two further questions. First of all, was the God conjured up at the coronation the true God or just some invention of the political Establishment? There have been many kings in history, a Christian would maintain, crowned in the name of many a false God.

It is certainly the case that the God of the coronation was the Protestant version. The undertakings the Queen had to make were, by today's ecumenical standards, most politically incorrect. First of all, she did 'solemnly and sincerely in the presence of God profess...that I will...secure the Protestant succession to the Throne of my Realm'. Then came this interrogation from the Archbishop of Canterbury:

'Will you to the utmost of your power maintain the Laws of God and the true profession of the Gospel? Will you to the utmost of your power maintain in the United Kingdom the Protestant Reformed Religion established by law? Will you maintain and preserve inviolably the settlement of the Church of England, and the doctrine, worship, discipline and government thereof, as by law established in England? And will you preserve unto the Bishops and Clergy of England, and to the Churches there committed to their charge, all such rights and privileges, as by law do or shall appertain to them or any of them?'

The Queen duly assented, then laid her right hand on the Bible and made this Solemn Oath, 'The things which I have here promised, I will perform and keep. So help me God.'

Roman Catholics can certainly wonder if indeed God's name was not being taken in vain.

The second question is rather different. Assuming that the God who sanctioned the coronation of Elizabeth II was the one true God, were the oaths administered in his name and the undertakings made in his presence binding for life? At the sacrament of marriage the vows most certainly are, but are the coronation oaths of a similar sacramental standing? The Dean of Westminster, the Very Reverend Dr A. C. Don, had no doubt at the time that they were for life, but to substantiate his view he had to turn to the Queen's own words uttered outside the Abbey in her declaration of six years earlier.

'I declare before you all that my whole life, whether it be long or short, shall be devoted to your service and the service of the great imperial family to which we all belong. But I shall not have strength to carry out this resolution alone, unless you join in it with me, as I now invite you to do. God help me to make good my vow, and God bless all of you who are willing to share it with me.'

Even those words are open to more than one interpretation. Suppose the Queen was shown that the greatest service she could render was to abdicate. Presumably her words of 1947 would not preclude her from doing so, no more than they precluded her from allowing her ministers to dismantle the last remnants of the Empire, her 'great imperial family'.

For practical purposes, however, in a modern secular society, the two pillars of authority, the Grace of God and the Will of the People, are inseparable. However firmly convinced a Monarch might believe that he or she reigns by the Grace of God, if the people no longer accept this, whether validly or not, then the position of the Monarch is untenable and his or her conviction of divine authority might as well be a delusion.

# 2

## *Majesty and Mystery*

The coronation of Queen Elizabeth II in 1953 was undeniably a magnificent public spectacle. As well as being a heart-warming event for a people still only just emerging from post-war rationing and for whom the consumer society was just a fanciful dream, it was also a superbly orchestrated public relations exercise. That it was a traditional ceremony with deep historic roots is undoubtedly true, but it was also a coronation for a modern age and designed for mass consumption. For no coronation has ever before been so public, and probably few if any have ever been so smoothly run.

Looking back at some of the coronations of history, there have been some major disasters and embarrassments. There was considerable confusion when Queen Victoria was crowned in 1838. At one point near the end of the service, one of the Queen's escorting bishops turned over two pages of his service book, thought he had come to the end of the ceremony, and led the Queen into St Edward's Chapel. The mistake however was spotted by the Sub-Dean of Westminster who informed the Prime Minister, and the Queen was duly summonsed again from the chapel to continue with the coronation.

In her journal, Queen Victoria wrote of Archbishop Howley that he was 'as usual confused, puzzled and knew nothing'. Amongst other errors, the Archbishop solemnly placed the ring on the wrong finger. Confiding in her journal again, the Queen wrote that she had the greatest difficulty taking it off again, 'which I at last did with great pain'. When everything was over, the Archbishop of Canterbury is reported to have said that he wished there had been a rehearsal.

In law, the Monarch takes on the mantle of power from the moment of accession. A coronation as the excuse for a great public spectacle to reinforce the monarchy is largely an invention of the twentieth century. It could be said that as the Monarch's powers have diminished so the need to provide ceremony to endorse them has grown. When sixteenth-century monarchs were crowned in Westminster Abbey, there was often just a small gathering of bishops and peers with the banquet in Westminster Hall being the main display of wealth and power. Two centuries later, coronations had grown in size but had become more confused in their execution. The Sword of State went missing before the coronation of George III, setting a good precedent for the muddles which were to be the most memorable feature of his grand-daughter's coronation in 1838.

Perhaps a coronation as a major spectacle for the masses had to wait for the age of the photograph and film. There are just a few grainy black and white cinema pictures of the dignitaries of state surviving from the coronation of Edward VII. George VI's coronation was filmed in all its glory using the latest cinematography, and television shots were transmitted to the tiny minority of the population who could afford the early sets. By 1953, the television age proper was dawning, and film makers had both colour and black-and-white stock at their disposal.

Thus it was that all people could see for the first time the solemnity of the day, and the ceremonies and formulae of words, once the preserve of the select, became public property.

And what did the public make of it all? What meaning did the ceremonial have for them? What was the atmosphere of the day?

Writing in the *Sociological Review* in December of that year, Edward Shils and Michael Young embellished an academic view with some colourful prose. They talked of the 'transformation of the frail creature' of Elizabeth II into a Queen at the moment of her crowning. This provided the essence of the drama of the coronation. They took the view that the theme of transformation remains one of the most basic and persistent human myths, forming the universal essence of fairy-stories, tribal ceremonies and the most elaborate religious exercises and beliefs.

Cinderella is transformed into a princess, and the beast into a prince. Leopard men take on the attributes of the animal they worship, and sinners are miraculously made Christian saints through the intervention of the mystic love of God.

The writers took the view that in Westminster Abbey on that morning in June, the House of Windsor finally perfected its own greatest transformation scene before the television cameras. This transformation would henceforth form the basis of its unshakeable mystique and universal fascination, as this 'familiar young woman, who for years had typified the simplest virtues of British girlhood and young womanhood, was recreated Queen in a moment of intense emotion'.

And in all the ceremonial, particularly at that moment of crowning, undoubtedly the key figures in the Abbey were the dignitaries of the Church. There were to be none of the undignified histrionics attendant at the crowning of Napoleon as Emperor when he upstaged the clerics, snatched the crown from the Papal Legate and placed it on his own head himself. Elizabeth II became the obedient servant of her Mother Church as it sanctified the occasion of her coronation and she renewed her dutiful pledges to her people.

'The Archbishop of Canterbury is the central figure, who officiates throughout,' wrote Dean Don, 'as his predecessors have had the right to do ever since the reign of William the Conqueror. He appoints two of his episcopal brethren to read the Epistle and the Gospel respectively ... The Archbishop of York has no claim to participate though he naturally takes his place in front of the Archbishop of Canterbury in the great procession.'

The majority of people who took part in the 1953 coronation, and certainly all the ecclesiastical dignitaries, are now dead. The peers, the bishops and the Government Minister attending were by and large Victorians, born in the reign of Queen Elizabeth's great-great-grandmother. Yet a vivid picture of the day emerges from newsreels, television recordings, photographs and written accounts.

Eight thousand people crammed into the Abbey for the occasion. Hundreds of thousands of people remained on the streets outside to see the coronation procession, and millions watched on television, perhaps seeing for the first time in their lives the television screen which was to dominate family life in the years to come.

While television viewers could not, of course, distinguish colours on their tiny black-and-white screens, those present in the Abbey, and those who later watched the cinema newsreels, witnessed a place of worship ablaze with colour. There was blue carpet, there were red and gold uniforms, and the rich purples of privilege and wealth. For her coronation, the Queen was supported by two bishops, and taking her place on the throne she sat on the mystical Stone of Scone. That stone, wrote Sir Harold Nicolson in his book *Monarchy*, represented 'the prehistoric element of magic'. It was the stone on which the kings of Scotland were crowned known as the stone of destiny which had been stolen by King Edward I and brought to Westminster to be inserted beneath the coronation chair.

In fact, the stone (which had been stolen only eighteen months before by some enterprising Scottish undergraduates) may not have been the genuine article at all, or if it was, Nicolson wonders whether its 'few weeks concealment in Scotland had materially diminished the stone's Palaeolithic magic'.

Nicolson describes the other elements of the coronation in this way:

The element of magic is also reflected in the extraordinary ritual...The Queen is acclaimed with all the pomp of great temporal sovereign; she is at the same time dedicated, almost as a sacrificial victim, to the service of her God and her peoples. There she sits clad in a tunic of cloth of gold, solitary and humble, modest and majestic, lonely and yet encompassed by the dignitaries of State and Church, aloof and detached, an Iphigenia dedicated to the welfare of her realm.

The king-priest element is also suggested by the service. The Queen is dressed in sacerdotal robes, in cope and stole; she moves slowly backwards and forwards across the theatre to the sound of anthems and the shouts of welcoming acolytes; she holds a Bible in her hand. The Church proclaims her its servant and she kneels humbly to the ministrations of the Church. The ritual is predominantly ecclesiastical; deliberately the monarch becomes a hierophant [a sacred symbol].

The anointing, which is regarded by the Church as the supreme ceremony of the Coronation, implies that, even as Zadok the priest and Nathan the prophet anointed Solomon, so also are the monarchs of England anointed by the heads of the Church. From the ampulla, the Dean of Westminster pours a few drops of oil into the spoon which he hands to the Archbishop. The Archbishop then anoints the Queen upon her head, her hands and her breast. From then on the Queen becomes 'the Lord's anointed': her person is holy.

The Coronation ends with the purely feudal rite of homage. The dukes, the earls, the barons kneel before her, promising to become her 'Liege man of Life and Limb and of earthly worship'.

In his commentary on the coronation written for the *Illustrated London News*, the Dean of Westminster described the liturgical framework of the coronation as being similar to that of the consecration of a bishop, especially in that it took place within the context of a service of Holy Communion.

After the Creed the Archbishop begins the ancient hymn, '*Veni Creator Spiritus*,' invoking the inspiration of the Holy Spirit. At this point, while the Queen kneels at a faldstool, she is stripped of her crimson robe and sits unadorned and expectant, awaiting her hallowing. After a prayer beginning 'O Lord, Holy Father, Who by anointing with oil didst of old make and consecrate Kings, Priests and Prophets to teach and govern Thy people Israel,' there follows the central act of the whole religious ceremony, the Unction, whereby the Queen is 'anointed, blessed and consecrated' to her high office. Four Knights of the Garter hold over her a canopy of cloth-of-gold, almost concealing her from sight. The Dean of Westminster brings from the Altar the Ampulla filled with oil, some of which he pours into the Spoon (probably the most ancient of all the Regalia). The Archbishop, dipping his finger in the oil, goes beneath the canopy and anoints the Queen in the form of a cross, thus signing her with the Sign of the Cross, as in baptism, 'in token that hereafter she shall not be ashamed to confess the faith of Christ crucified, and manfully to fight under his banner against sin, the world and the devil, and to continue Christ's faithful soldier and servant unto her life's end.' Indeed, in mediaeval times, as the Canonist Lindwood expresses it, an anointed King or Queen was regarded as '*mixta persona*,' half-ecclesiastic and half-laic, possessed of an inalienable and ineffaceable 'character,' so that 'Not all the water in the rough rude sea can wash the balm off from an anointed King'.

As an accompaniment to this, the most sacred of all the Coronation rites, the choir sing to the glorious music of Handel (composed for the Coronation of George II) the words taken from the First Book of Kings which, from time immemorial, have formed part of the Coronation ritual: 'Zadok the priest, and Nathan the prophet, anointed Solomon King. And all the people rejoiced and said: *God*

*save the King; Long live the King; May the King live for ever.
Amen. Hallelujah.'*

The Unction comes thus early in the service for the reason that it is only by virtue of her anointing that the Queen
is qualified and entitled to receive into her hands the
emblems of her royal estate, and to assume the robes befit-
ting her newly-bestowed dignity.

The images of the anointed monarch come from the Old Testament, in 1 Kings 1:32–40, quoted here in the words of the
Authorized Version.

And king David said, Call me Zadok the priest, and Nathan
the prophet, and Benaiah the son of Jehoiada. And they
came before the king.

The king also said unto them, Take with you the servants
of your lord, and cause Solomon my son to ride upon mine
own mule, and bring him down to Gihon:

And let Zadok the priest and Nathan the prophet anoint
him there king over Israel: and blow ye with the trumpet,
and say, God save king Solomon.

Then ye shall come up after him, that he may come and
sit upon my throne; for he shall be king in my stead: and I
have appointed him to be ruler over Israel and over Judah.

And Benaiah the son of Jehoiada answered the king, and
said, Amen: the LORD God of my lord the king say so too.

As the LORD hath been with my lord the king, even so be
he with Solomon, and make his throne greater than the
throne of my lord king David.

So Zadok the priest, and Nathan the prophet, and Benaiah the son of Jehoiada, and the Cherethites, and the
Pelethites, went down, and caused Solomon to ride upon
king David's mule, and brought him to Gihon.

And Zadok the priest took an horn of oil out of the taber-
nacle, and anointed Solomon. And they blew the trumpet;
and all the people said, God save king Solomon.

And all the people came up after him, and the people
piped with pipes, and rejoiced with great joy, so that the
earth rent with the sound of them.

Archbishop Fisher is on record as claiming that the anointing of
the Monarch is the central and most significant ritual in the whole
coronation ceremony.

In his book *The Crowning of Elizabeth II*, L. A. Nickolls also
emphasized the centrality in the coronation service of the Holy
Communion. The rite used was that of the historic Book of
Common Prayer, and the whole reverent majesty of the estab-
lished Church, of which the Queen was supreme governor on
earth, was paraded before the congregation and nation. The
Epistle was read by the Bishop of London, and the Gospel by the
Archbishop of York.

Nickolls quoted more of the Archbishop's words uttered during that personal and sacred rite of anointing, the only part of the
whole service, it was felt by the Queen and her advisers, into
which the television cameras should be forbidden to pry.

'Be thy Head anointed with holy Oil: as kings, priests, and
prophets were anointed. And as Solomon was anointed king
by Zadok the priest and Nathan the prophet, so be thou
anointed, blessed, and consecrated Queen over the People,
whom the Lord thy God hath given thee to rule and govern, In the Name of the Father, and of the Son, and of the
Holy Ghost. Amen.'

Then the Queen temporarily left the Coronation Chair to
go to a faldstool in the sanctuary, where she knelt to receive
the Archbishop's blessing, at the end of which she returned
to the Chair while the Knights of the Garter withdrew with
the Canopy. There was a pause before the next part of the

ceremony – the investiture with the Colobium Sindonis and the Supertunica with Girdle. These shimmering garments, almost dazzling under the powerful lamps that reinforced the daylight streaming in from the rose windows in each transept, were of cloth of gold. After the Dean and the Mistress of the Robes had adjusted them, the Queen stood for a few moments – a figure of beauty and regal splendour, flashing with gold – before she again took her seat in the Coronation Chair.

Thus accoutred in royal glory, the Queen was ready to receive all the other insignia of her estate. From this point onward the investiture proceeded at quicker pace. First there were the Spurs – a touch on the hands from them, as they were presented by the Lord Great Chamberlain – and next came the ceremony of the Sword. At the Altar the Sword of State was exchanged for the Jewelled Sword, its scabbard showing the emblems of the Kingdom set in a pattern of diamonds, rubies, emeralds, and as he delivered it to the Queen, the Archbishop said:

'Receive this kingly Sword, brought now from the Altar of God, and delivered to you by the hands of us the Bishops and servants of God, though unworthy...'

At first the Queen held the Sword point upward. Then she lowered it till it rested horizontally across her outstretched hands. Thus she walked to the Altar, clad in gold, while the lights shimmered on her as she slowly entered the sanctuary. She handed the Sword to the Dean, who was beside the Altar, and after she had resumed her seat in the Coronation Chair, Lord Salisbury, whose part this day was that of Sword Bearer, went to the Altar to redeem the Sword for the traditional gift of a hundred shillings. On receiving the Sword from the Dean, he drew it from its scabbard, and thereafter, throughout the remainder of the ceremony, he carried it naked, with point upward.

The pageantry of installation moved swiftly towards the climax – the Crowning. The Archbishops gave to the Queen

the Armills – golden bracelets provided by the Commonwealth Governments in revival of Coronation insignia
neglected since the Stuarts. Then came the 'Garments of
Salvation', comprising the Stole Royal and the Robe Royal,
the clasps of which were fastened by the Lord Great Chamberlain. Next there was the Orb, placed by the Archbishop
in the right hand of the Queen, who later delivered it to the
Dean; then there was the Ring, slipped on to the fourth finger of her right hand by the Archbishop; then the Glove of
embroidered white kid, brought by Lord Woolton; and
finally, as the last act before the Crowning, the Archbishop
delivered into her right hand the Sceptre with the Cross and
into her left hand the Rod with the Dove – the Sceptre as an
ensign of kingly power and justice, the Rod as an emblem of
equity and mercy.

As the young Queen meticulously and flawlessly performed each
ritual, what did she truly make of it? Was she simply acting a part
as an actress on a stage or did she actually believe what was being
said about her and performed in her name? In his book *Majesty*,
published in 1977, Robert Lacey gave this assessment:

Queen Elizabeth II's view of her own function in the
summer of 1953 was infused with mysticism. Early in her
adolescence she had experienced her parents' devout consecration and now she dedicated herself with similar zeal.
'Pray for me on that day,' she asked in the first Christmas
broadcast of her reign in December 1952. 'Pray that God
may give me wisdom and strength to carry out the solemn
promises I shall be making.' The Archbishop of Canterbury,
Geoffrey Fisher, had prepared a programme of daily read-
ings and meditations to lead up to the ceremony, and on the
day itself, reported Dermot Morrah who, as a Herald, stood
near the throne, 'the sense of spiritual exultation that radiat-
ed from her was almost tangible'.

A *Times* leader described how the Queen had stood 'for the soul as well as the body of the Commonwealth'.

It is interesting to note that unlike the first Queen Elizabeth, the present queen did not retire from the abbey to a robing room for the Communion and unlike Queen Victoria, Queen Elizabeth II accepted full anointing. In the interests of modesty, her great-great-grandmother was not anointed on the breast.

The meticulously executed ceremonial of the coronation, with its visual splendour and with the solemnity of its religious language, could scarcely fail to make a deep impression on the new Queen's subjects. Through what they witnessed on television, the whole nation was encouraged simultaneously to feel an intense involvement with their young Queen and to reverence the monarchy as an awesome, divinely sanctioned institution.

Indeed, such was the universal acclaim for the new Elizabethan age that for years following the coronation there was hardly anyone in the country who dared speak out against the monarchy. Possibly it is wrong to say 'dared', for the lack of any public criticism of the Monarch stemmed not so much from a lack of courage but the absence of a critical voice. Even the socialist Members of Parliament took their seats in the Abbey. Typical of the praise lavished on the institution was that of the former Labour party politician Herbert Morrison, writing in 1954. In his book, entitled *Government and Parliament*, he wrote:

Not withstanding the fact that the crown has lost its original great powers it can be said, certainly of the present century, that as those powers past and the monarchy became strictly constitutional, the monarch has become increasingly popular in the hearts and minds of the British people. No monarchy in the world is more secure or more respected by the people than ours. The steady increase in the esteem of the nation for King George V and King George VI was something of which we are all aware. The welcome to the young

Queen Elizabeth II was real and sincere and her coronation in 1953 became a great national festival. Wherever she goes she is assured of a great and genuine welcome. When the people cheer the queen and sing her praises, they are also cheering our free democracy.

Not a hint there of the carping criticism which can be found for the Monarch at all levels in society today. There was no suggestion then that she should pay income tax, or that she was aloof and remote, or that her wealth was too extravagant and her properties too vast and in total disproportion to the individual wealth of most of her subjects.

Herbert Morrison attributed the security and popularity of the British monarchy largely to the fact that it did not govern and that government was the task of Ministers responsible to a House of Commons elected by the people. 'The monarchy as it exists,' Morrison argued, 'now facilitates the processes of parliamentary democracy and functions as an upholder of freedom and representative government.'

There will be many political observers today who take the view that Parliament has been superseded itself by the executive, elected once every five years, at a time to suit its own advantage and which, provided it has a paper majority in the House of Commons, is able to disregard the views and opinions of backbenchers and the electorate. In addition, much power has passed from Parliament, which in the old days could scrutinize the accounts and activities of the nationalized industries, to privatized monopolies and quangos where members, loyal to the ruling party and dependent on its patronage, exercise vast power at grassroots level. Again, back in 1954, Herbert Morrison was able to write – and few would have disagreed – 'nowadays there are not many republicans in our country'.

It was the supposed political impartiality of the Crown which attracted Herbert Morrison and others.

If [the Crown] continues to be strictly impartial, to be ani-
mated by a high sense of public duty, it will continue to
achieve its almost universal popularity.

It is not for me to pronounce upon the merits of the republican regimes in France, in the United States or elsewhere: that
is the business of the nations concerned. But for our country
constitutional monarchy is a success and deserves the support
and respect which it undoubtedly receives from the people.

With hindsight, it can perhaps be argued that that period around
the end of the Second World War surviving for another 10 or 15
years well into the reign of Queen Elizabeth II, was an exceptional high spot in the fortunes of the monarchy. Certainly at the
time of Edward VII, Edward VIII and for long spells during the
reign of Queen Victoria – let alone during the periods of
debauchery and dispute which marked much of the Hanoverian
era – the Monarch was held in low esteem.

Writing in the 1860s during the reign of Queen Victoria, the
constitutionalist Walter Bagehot put a slant on the English Constitution which has been quoted ever since. It was he who put into
words the legend of the impartial Monarch doing his or her duty
for the benefit of the people and the preservation of democracy.

The sovereign has three rights – to be consulted, to encourage and to warn. And a king of great sense and sagacity
would want no others. He would find that his having no
others would enable him to use these with singular effect.
He would say to his minister: 'The responsibility of these
measures is upon you. Whatever you think best must be
done. Whatever you think best shall have my full and effectual support. But you will observe that for this reason and
that reason what you propose to do is bad; for this reason
and that reason what you do not propose is better. I do not
oppose, it is my duty not to oppose: But observe that I
warn.' Supposing the king to be right, and to have what

kings often have, the gift of effectual expression, he could not help moving his minister. He might not always turn his course, but he would always trouble his mind.

In the course of a long reign a sagacious king would acquire an experience with which few ministers could contend. The minister could say: 'Have you referred to the transactions which happened during such and such administration, I think about fourteen years ago? They afford an instructive example of the bad results which are sure to attend the policy which you propose. You did not at that time take so prominent a part in public life as you do now, and it is possible you do not fully remember all the events.'

By the 1890s when the Duke of York, later King George V, was receiving instruction in the law and practice of the constitution the story is told of the summary he wrote and which was later recorded in the biography *King George V, His Life and Reign* by Sir Harold Nicolson.

Sir Harold Nicolson quoted the summary having observed that the Duke was required by his tutors to read Bagehot. The summary of the duties of the monarch included the following.

The value of the crown in its dignified capacity. a) It makes government intelligible to the masses. b) It makes government interesting to the masses. c) It strengthens government with the religious tradition connected with the crown.

At this point it was noted that after the accession of George III the Hanoverians inherited the traditional reverence of Stuart times. The summary then went on to talk of the social value of the Crown and the moral value. 'Great for good or evil.'

The present Queen's own constitutional schooling in the 1940s continued to rely on Bagehot, despite the fact that he had been writing in an era well before mass communication and universal suffrage. From her very first broadcast as a Princess, she dedicated herself to duty and, like her great-great-grandmother Queen Victoria, to 'being good'.

Even 70 years after the then Duke of York wrote his summary, the description of the constitutional Monarch, as based on Bagehot, still formed the standard understanding of the role of the Monarch. In the text book, *Politics in England*, published in the early sixties, Richard Rose wrote:

> The Queen is the most prominent symbol in the political system. As Head of State, the Queen performs many ceremonial functions that regularly involve her though only as a figurehead in the workings of government and invest these workings with some of the monarch's aura...
>
> Through the Queen's dual position of Head of State and Defender of the Faith, the government is linked to religion and the sources of religious authority. The strength of emotional attitudes towards the monarch is indicated by the attacks upon those who occasionally criticize the Queen – and also by the rarity of criticism along Republican lines.

Richard Rose's observation could not have been better illustrated than by the episode of Lord Altrincham who, in August 1957, wrote an article about the monarchy in an edition of the *National and English Review*.

He dared criticize the style of the current monarch and indignant reaction followed immediately. Yet he was very careful himself not to attack the Queen, knowing even then that that was beyond the pale, but to question the suitability of some of her advisers. He suggested that the Queen's entourage 'are almost without exception the "tweedy" sort'. He also argued that the Buckingham Palace hierarchy had 'lamentably failed to live with the times. While the monarchy has become "popular" and multi-racial the court has remained a tight little enclave of English ladies and gentlemen.' While protesting his loyalty, he did make further points, claiming them to be put in the Queen's best interest.

When she has lost the bloom of youth, the Queen's reputation will depend, far more than it does now, upon her personality. It will not then be enough for her to go through the motions: She will have to say things which people can remember and do things on her own initiative which will make people sit up and take notice. As yet there is little sign that such a personality is emerging.

Not only did the Establishment sharply criticize the peer for poor form and poor judgement, he was even given a slap by an elderly ardent monarchist in front of the television cameras.

Interestingly, however, when one newspaper polled its younger readers (those under the age of 35), a majority agreed with Lord Altrincham by a ratio of 39:47, and that within all groups in society it was felt that the court circle around the Queen should and could be extended.

Later, in Robert Lacey's *Majesty*, John Grigg, Lord Altrincham, was quoted as blaming the 1957 storm on the 'Shintoistic atmosphere of the post-coronation period...there was a tendency – quite alien to our national tradition – to regard as high treason any criticism of the monarch however loyal and constructive its intent'. By the late sixties, Lord Altrincham's views about the remoteness of the Queen had become almost mainstream. In *Anatomy of Britain Today*, Anthony Sampson wrote:

The remoteness of the Queen is enhanced by her entourage. Most of her time is spent with people who, from the public's point of view, are in a half-and-half world between royalty and ordinariness. Many of the guests at Windsor or Balmoral have titles, and Dukes, particularly racing Dukes, make up the foothills to royalty.

What is interesting to note is that barely a dozen years after her coronation Queen Elizabeth II was beginning to lose the hard-won esteem and affection which she had inherited from her father. For what endeared King George VI and his wife Queen Elizabeth to the British people was that they did not seem remote from them. They stayed in London during the Blitz so that, in Queen Elizabeth's words, 'she could look the eastenders in the eye'. They were still royal and in many ways still remote and mysterious, but they were careful to appear to have a genuine empathy with the people. Queen Elizabeth, now the Queen Mother, is still the only member of the royal family for whom it can be claimed there is a universal affection. She is now of great age and cannot be expected to live for many more years, and once she is gone there will be no one left in the family with whom the whole British people feel an affectionate bond.

Anthony Sampson's chapter on the Palace also took a text from Walter Bagehot, who had written of the monarchy, 'its mystery is its life. We must not let in daylight upon magic.' Sampson went on:

The problem of how to keep the fairyland under control has caused some worry to the palace. Already before the war, the monarchy had taken over a quasi-religious position. 'In the middle of the last century,' wrote Kingsley Martin in 1937, 'it needed courage to break the religious taboo, to doubt the literal truth of the first chapter of Genesis, or question the scientific basis for belief in the Virgin birth. The throne on the other hand was frankly criticised in the newspapers and on the platform. In the 20th century the situation is exactly reversed.

It is hard now imagining *The Times* commenting, as they did on the funeral of King George IV, 'there never was an individual less regretted by his fellow creatures than this deceased king'.

After the war, and with the end of secrecy, and with the royal wedding and the royal baby, public excitement began to reach alarming proportions: and with the coronation in 1953 public adoration seemed to have got out of control –

like a captive balloon that had broken loose from its mooring. The public frenzy continued, watched by some palace officials with growing bewilderment, and an uneasy feeling that the balloon might eventually hit something and explode: but in the past few years there have been some signs that the public interest has been moderating, only partly revived by the crop of royal babies in 1964. Malcolm Muggeridge complained to an American television audience in February 1964: 'The story goes on and on. There is the happy family, there was a problem sister, and now all the girls are going to have babies. Here are all the ingredients of a soap opera. The English were getting bored with their monarchy. I think it is coming to an end.'

So it was that, from the 1960s onwards, the Palace had a public relations problem. In public esteem, the House of Windsor had risen to ludicrous heights. It had nowhere to go but down.

# 3

# *A Fading Romance*

Fearing that the mystery of the monarchy would sooner or later fail, the Palace took a step which flew in the face of Bagehot's warning that 'We must not let in daylight upon magic'. It was decided that a veil would be lifted on the royal mystery – the people would be given the opportunity to see something of the family at work. It was thought, much in the way that it is thought by the scriptwriters of soap operas today, that if the plots become too predictable and the cast too familiar something is required to spice the programme up or the ratings fall.

It was felt inconceivable that the monarch would fall again to such depths of public loathing as the later Hanoverians had experienced. No one even contemplated that the pendulum would swing back that far. After all, the monarchy had this century acquired what Kingsley Martin had described as a quasi-religious position.

The Palace decided to allow the television cameras to follow the royal family around and produce a documentary to be broadcast around the time of Prince Charles's investiture as Prince of Wales. The production of the programme was a very carefully monitored and controlled exercise, as Jonathan Dimbleby describes in his biography of Prince Charles.

As preparations for the investiture were finalised, viewers of BBC television were treated to the first-ever glimpse behind the royal tableau to witness the Queen and her family 'off duty'. The documentary 'Royal Family' was conceived by William Heseltine, working closely with John Brabourne, as a means of using television to show the public a little of the life the Prince would eventually be expected to lead as the future sovereign and of the preparations that were being made for him to fulfil that role. Working under the overall control of a committee chaired by Prince Philip, the BBC producer Richard Cawston was given unprecedented access to the family and to the household. The film showed Prince Philip barbecuing sausages, the Queen washing up, and Prince Edward and Andrew having a snowball fight at Sandringham. Later, those critics who blamed the Palace for allowing the monarchy to be turned into a 'soap opera' would cite 'Royal Family' as the first step down a disastrous slope which led directly to the nadir of 'It's A Royal Knockout'.

Whatever the royal family hoped to achieve by making the film, it did not have any long-term effect on the very slow and gradual fall of the House of Windsor.

Bit by bit, the press became bolder in its coverage of the family's fortunes. There were high spots on the way when royal weddings were held, and low spots as Princess Anne's personality was put under the spotlight for a while and was found to be sharp and petulant. The delightful Princess Margaret Rose, the family's publicity dream child in the thirties and forties, became 'that expensive kept woman'.

Princess Margaret is probably now the most resented member of the Windsor family, having lived at public expense all her life and continuing to insist haughtily on being treated with due respect to her rank. In his book *Inside Kensington Palace*, Andrew Morton wrote this sketch of a day in the life of the Countess of Snowdon. Given his track-record for uncovering the intimate details of Palace life, his description is unlikely to be far wide of the mark.

The Princess's day starts very quietly at eleven o'clock when her jolly housekeeper, Liz Greenfield, takes up a tray of tea – Lapsang Suchong served in Spode china – to her bedroom. After she has dressed and read her mail she will call for a cup of very strong black Brazilian blend coffee. She takes it everywhere with her. When she travels on a Queen's flight a silver flask of her favourite coffee from the Nairobi Coffee Company goes with her.

There is no rigid pattern to her day. In the late morning she may go out with a friend to watch a ballet rehearsal, meet her private secretary to discuss any royal business or spend an hour shopping. Her secretary, Muriel Murray-Brown, spends much of the morning organizing guests for lunch.

Every Monday Princess Margaret goes through the week's menu. Her menu card, printed at Buckingham Palace, offers her a similar choice to that presented to the Queen and the Queen Mother...

After lunch Princess Margaret, who has between three and four engagements a week, is usually on duty, sweeping down the drive with her motorcycle escort, the 'Black Rats'...

The Princess enjoys the company of others, and it is a rare night indeed that she dines in alone. When that happens she eats from a tray and watches television. Even then she likes to have people around her. One evening while watching the film 'Superman' she saw with delight that some of the many places she had visited were featured. She summoned her long-serving, and long-suffering, butler John Leighman to share her enjoyment. While she sat watching the film, pointing out places of interest, he was forced to stand there and make polite conversation. He was itching to sit down but could only do so when she commanded it. The command was never given.

Thankfully however the Princess is invariably out in the evening. She stays out so late that she is the only member of the royal family to carry a front door key, but she is always losing them. At home she enjoys hosting a formal dinner party. Asparagus or salmon are usually served first, with fillet of beef for the main course followed by a cold dessert. Before one dinner party where the entertainers John Dankworth and Cleo Laine were guests of honour, Dankworth's secretary rang to inform the Princess that he was vegetarian and that he could not eat any meat. Princess Margaret saw red; she would not be dictated to. Meat, and lots of it, was featured on the menu that night.

Inevitably some of his mother's attitudes have rubbed off on Viscount Linley. Morton tells the story of how he was spotted by one of the staff lavishing attention on a much cherished car.

Just to pass the time of day the servant commented: 'I bet it will rain now you have washed it.' Linley gave him a blank look. 'Are you talking to me?' he replied. 'Yes,' said the servant. 'Call me sir,' said Linley abruptly and started cleaning his car again. 'Come the revolution,' muttered the servant as he went on his way, smarting from the insult.

Even the Windsors themselves must have been forced to acknowledge that with certain royals being consistently low in public esteem they were all liable to fall in the royal popularity charts.

Iindividual members of the royal family were undoubtedly popular, or at least more acceptable than others. But, gradually, a universal feeling of discontent emerged. It was seldom put into words but amounted to this – that the wealth and privilege of the royal family had cut them off from the people. Today, the Queen and her subjects have no experiences in common and no real empathy exists between them. Over two decades when the rich have apparently become richer and the poor have become poorer, the Queen's wealth has grown. As one of the very richest, even though now she has reluctantly agreed to pay income tax on her private wealth, her fortune has shown no signs of decline. Indeed, over the centuries, she has become almost unique in her position as a wealthy aristocrat. Few other peers of ancient title can claim to be so wealthy. Even a hundred years ago, before death duties and other taxation ate into their estates, there were a number of aristocrats who could live in the same style as the monarch. They had grand palaces and kept retinues of servants. They were like monarchs in their own realm. This is no longer the case and the Queen, although being rivalled in wealth by the Duke of Westminster, is the only super-aristocrat left.

While in her private life she may have fits of unnecessary parsimony and belt-tightening, publicly, her lifestyle is still immensely costly to maintain. And what is perhaps most resented by the British people are the lifestyles of some of the hangers-on. What does Princess Margaret do to earn her keep? And then there are those like the Duchess of York who, it is considered, shamelessly flaunt their royal status for financial gain. There is no way that she would ever have sold her idea of a cartoon character called Budgie the Helicopter if she had not been a royal. Even if she had, the returns would have been very modest, nothing like the estimated £3 million it is thought it will earn, helping to wipe out her substantial debts.

Fergie is also the queen of the freebie. Her huge debts are now public knowledge. As the divorced wife of a member of the royal family she will remain a duchess until she re-marries, but she will have lost the much-coveted handle 'Her Royal Highness'. She attempts to sign deals to recoup money she owes. Perhaps she will in the end have to resort to a 'full and frank' autobiography – breaking undertakings she has made to the Windsors. If she is truly honest in her published recollections, such honesty can only damage both herself and the monarchy.

Yet it is unfair to spotlight Fergie, as all the royal family are adept at high-level scrounging. In his book *The Rise and Fall of the House of Windsor*, A. N. Wilson begins his chapter on royal money with this paragraph:

When Norman Hartnell, the Queen's dressmaker, died, there was a flurry among all the grand couturiers in London. Was this, I asked one of them, because they were all so anxious to make dresses for the Queen Mother and the Queen? Not at all. They all dreaded the commission. When I asked why, I was told that the Queen Mother had seldom been known to pay a bill in her life. 'The Queen, of course,' said my informant, 'pays on the nail. But we have not had the heart to tell her that prices have risen somewhat since 1947.'

Wilson readily concedes that if the House of Windsor has aroused envy and rancour in the populace at large it has to be partly because of its greed and its meanness.

It is perhaps a family trait. Traditionally, monarchs have always been money-grabbing; sometimes they have been so poor they have had to be. Many a row has been had between Monarch and Parliament, for Parliament is the body which raises the taxes. The debts of the Hanoverians were notorious; the Stuarts, too, were constantly at loggerheads with Parliament not just on religious issues but on the question of money as well. Of course, in those days, the Crown needed money from Parliament not just for personal expenses but also to govern. The King ran the Government, not just his own retinue.

Over the last century, however, the Monarch has been out of debt and has accumulated substantial wealth consisting of property, cash and priceless paintings. Nevertheless, the royals continued to raise the grabbing of the freebie to an art form. Householders dreaded visits by Queen Mary, it is said. She had a disconcerting habit of eyeing individual items, works of art and so on, and dropping heavy hints that she would like to be given them as a present. Often, a householder risked substantial royal disapproval if the object was not handed over to the lady-in-waiting.

King Edward VII and George V scrounged shamelessly on the shooting circuit. Jonathan Ruffer, writing in *The Field* in May

1995, wrote of Edward VII as Prince of Wales that he had invented the art form of inviting oneself to shoot on other people's estates. His particular forte was to encourage the newly ennobled families with wealth to set up extravagant shooting parties and then to invite him to the very best position in the hope that some of the regal approval would rub off on them and they would gain a higher position in society. Both King Edward VII and his son liked massacring birds in huge quantity. As a result, Ruffer writes 'the King had the best peg. It never occurred to anyone, least of all the monarch, that it should be otherwise...the result of this was that certain drives where the king shot regularly became known as the King's peg, such as Peg Number Three at the Sugar Loaf Drive at Eriswell, on the Elveden estate'.

Even George VI, whose public image has seldom been tarnished, was well practised in his father's and grandfather's art. Once, on a shoot, George VI was placed on the wrong flank and he ticked off his host, albeit in a bantering sort of way.

Much of the royal extravagance of course goes unnoticed and is absorbed into other bills the taxpayers meet. On royal tours, expenses claims are sent by the Monarch to the Embassy. These will often include small, everyday items, or even new clothes for the Monarch. In that way, they live off their expenses as well as receiving their annual allowances. The Prince of Wales, for instance, likes, as did his father, to take the control of an aircraft when he is travelling. This had costly results on one trip to the Hebrides. While the royals may be in control, playing at being pilots, there has to be substantial and costly expert back up.

Then there are the Royal Yacht and the Royal Train and the whole host of minor facilities which have to be kept on stand-by in case the Queen needs them. The future of the Royal Yacht is presently under review. It would appear likely that the opinion of one Labour MP that *Britannia* is 'a geriatric waste of money and should be retired as soon as possible' might in due course become generally accepted. A replacement would cost around

£80 million, a great deal of money for a facility which the royal family only uses less than two months a year.

Anthony Holden in his book *The Tarnished Crown* described *Britannia* in this way:

> *Britannia* is decorated in manor-house style, with oak panels, hand-woven rugs, antique chairs and hand-picked flowers from around the royal residences. While the royals are aboard, the crew wear a special uniform to show they are about royal duties: their jumpers are tucked inside their trousers, which are trimmed with a black silk bow. White-coated stewards are on round-the-clock duty to serve drinks and meals either in the royal cabins or in the elegant dining room, whose antique walnut table seats forty. The dining room doubles as private cinema with seating for twenty.
>
> The crew are trained to look away when a royal comes in sight. Silence is compulsory; the staff communicate by hand signals and wear rubber soles so as not to disturb the royal slumbers. 'The royal family are treated better on board *Britannia* than they are at the Palace,' said one former crew member. 'Everything has to be just right.' In the Caribbean, there was even a twenty-six-strong Royal Marines band on board for the royal princes' entertainment.

One ten-day cruise by Prince Philip in the Caribbean cost the taxpayer over £5 million. As Anthony Holden wrote, it was at the time 'when his wife's subjects were buckled beneath Norman Lamont's latest budget'. 'Philip must need his head examining,' said one Tory MP, in one of the milder and more polite rebukes. But this was by no means the sole occasion on which excessive sums have been spent on royal travel, as Holden points out.

Philip flew to meet *Britannia* aboard a British Aerospace 146 jet of the Queen's Flight (at a return cost to the taxpayer, as has been seen, of more than a dozen times the first-class return fare aboard British Airways). The royal fleet consists of three 146s bought by the Ministry of Defence for the Queen's Flight in 1986 for £16.4 million each, and two Wessex helicopters. They are used primarily by the Queen, Prince Philip and the Prince of Wales; other family members may use the aircraft only on royal business and with the Queen's permission. In 1993 the future of the Queen's Flight, like that of the royal yacht, was officially declared 'under review' by the Ministry of Defence, who had been asked to 'make savings'. One idea under discussion was to cut back the fleet to just one aircraft for official trips. Public criticism had grown since 1990, when Charles used one of his mother's jets to go skiing; the cost to the taxpayer was £20,000, compared with a commercial fare of less than £500. In March 1993, while his estranged wife flew by scheduled aircraft for an official aid visit to Nepal, Charles flew to another skiing holiday in Klosters in a jet of the Queen's Flight, which returned to collect him a week later.

Coupled with extravagance the royal family has also been guilty of an unbelievable insensitivity. Where was Prince Charles on the night that Prince William received emergency surgery for a fractured skull? According to Holden:

After an evening at the opera, Charles took the Royal Train to York overnight, to spend the next day showing European Commissioners around the East Riding 'wetlands'. He then flew home by Royal Flight. The train thus spent the night in a siding, before travelling back empty while an empty aircraft flew up to collect him. Charles's Yorkshire 'awayday', while his wife kept vigil at their son's hospital bedside, cost the British taxpayer in excess of £70,000.

That incident which yet further tarnished the image of the House of Windsor produced accusations not just of extravagance and a callous disregard for his son, but of hypocrisy as well. How could a prince who preached environmentalism and was so proud of his 'green' credentials have sanctioned such a waste of resources?

While the Queen does not go skiing, she does nevertheless indulge in her own expensive hobbies, keeping top-notch race horses being the best known. Yet her most wasteful activities concern her role as constitutional monarch. She commands ministers to attend on her and has State papers despatched to her wherever she is around the world and wastes hours of government time with absurd private ceremonies. The meetings of the Privy Council, when ministers of the Crown have to perform a pantomime more akin to freemasonry than good government, are among the most unnecessary and ridiculous. Former minister Alan Clark described one meeting in his famously indiscreet diaries. It was the occasion he was inducted as a Member of the Privy Council after which he would be entitled to be styled 'The Right Honourable'.

I stepped forward, knelt awkwardly on the stool (bloody difficult), held up the Testament in my right hand and the dear old boy read out the oath. 'I do,' I said, firmly. I rose, advanced about ten feet diagonally to *another* stool, bowed, knelt, took the Monarch's hand and 'brushed it with my lips'; rose, bowed, back into line.

A pause ensued. Why? I made to go forward, down the line, shake hands with the Lord President as forewarned and instructed. No. Blast, f**k, etc. There was *another* oath. The old Clerk, secretly delighted, rolled his eyes in mock resignation and signalled me to raise, again, the Testament in my right hand. He then read out a very long passage the substance of which, as far as I could make out, was that I undertook to maintain total secrecy even, particularly indeed, about colleagues concerning whom I might hear unsatisfactory things. (The more I think about this the odder it seems.)

This time, when I said 'I do' I looked directly at the Queen. I bet many don't. But I was glad to see that she was looking directly at me. I then did the handshaking act, Lord President, Attorney General, the rest, and returned to my place at the end of the line. At which the Queen got up from her chair and moved over, *regally*, to initiate a painfully, grotesquely, banal conversation, loosely devoted to the various other Orders in Council that were on the business list…

This last phase was somewhat drawn out. Not for the first time I wondered about the Queen. Is she really rather dull and stupid? Or is she thinking, 'How do people as dull and stupid as this ever get to be Ministers?' Or is, for her, the whole thing so stale and *déjà vu* after forty years that she'd really rather be going round the stables at Highclere, patting racehorses on the nose? I suppose it might feel different if she had real power. And yet she *does* have the power. It's all there in the Constitution, all she has to do is renounce the Civil List for her ill-favoured siblings, pay taxes on her private wealth, and get on with it.

All the private ceremonial in which the Queen indulges seems utterly pointless. It can in no way help enhance the magic of monarchy, for no one outside a privileged circle ever witnesses it. When her sight fails and her mind begins to wander in old age, her conscientious attention to the State boxes will no longer be required of her and no doubt Government will carry on as before. She has no power, so why should she tie up so much government time? Indeed, constitutional monarchs who dabble in the minutiae of government are found by elected representatives to be the most nuisance.

The Queen's supporters will no doubt argue that what little influence she can exercise, she exercises well. When a hoaxer from a Canadian radio station called her pretending to be his country's Prime Minister, she did not put a constitutional foot wrong, or so it is claimed. But assuming that were the case and she acted entirely properly and impartially, what a very small plus point that is, or so her detractors would say. By comparison, they would highlight the huge minus points of her reign. The most substantial minus point being that the Queen has been so privileged and quarantined from real life by her circle of courtiers that she has no point of contact with the real world in which her subjects inhabit. What advice can she give to elected politicians worried over poverty, state education, unemployment and injustice? She has no first-hand experience of any of these things. On the few occasions she is shown on television meeting ordinary people, she is painfully socially inadequate, such has been the complete protection afforded her during almost her entire life.

Unfortunately, too, she has never developed a warm or approachable method of public speaking. Her latest biographer, Sarah Bradford, believes she has also lacked both confidence and ability.

'She was not very good about speeches,' an aide said. 'Not a natural composer of them. Relied a good deal on Prince Philip. The draft would be put up by one of the private secretaries and then she would alter it, or rather Prince Philip would.'

'She's a very honest person. It's difficult to make her say something or quote something particular unless she really knows about it,' another said. 'For instance, if you suggested she should say "We are very pleased to be here in Hull today", she would cross out the "very".'

Since she doesn't find speaking easy, Elizabeth always reads her speeches, which contributes even more to the general impression of lack of spontaneity which she gives. She just cannot memorise the words or improvise, any more than her mother does. Maybe it is inherited. There is a story, perhaps apocryphal, of Queen Mary going to the launch of the liner the SS Queen Mary, and telling her lady-in-waiting beforehand, 'Oh dear, I'm sure I'm not going to remember the name.'

Queen Elizabeth knows no other life than that which revolves around the perks and duties of being a Windsor. The royals have private access to the country's best sporting facilities, one of its finest art collections, as well as a choice of some of the finest houses in the country to live in. Balmoral, Sandringham, Windsor Castle – depending on the time of year and which lengthy period of holiday the family is enjoying.

And do the royals appreciate all this? It is certainly said they enjoy the country pursuits, but as for anything else, royal observers generally regard Elizabeth as a Philistine. She practically never reads a book unless it is horse-related. She does not enjoy the opera, theatre or concerts – not even ballet, for which her mother and sister are enthusiasts. Science and technology bore her. Philip is credited with having told someone who suggested the Queen might like to visit a high-tech plant: 'Unless it eats grass and farts, she isn't interested.'

A little unfair, perhaps – but not much. In this seeming indifference to much of what her privilege offers, she is little different from many of her forebears who took so much of their wealth for granted. When Windsor Castle was partially destroyed by fire it cannot be doubted that the Queen was genuinely distressed to see so much of her heritage destroyed. Perhaps the blow was somewhat softened by an assumption that much of it would be restored. One of the most unpleasant moments in her *annus horribilis* must have come when she realized that such an assumption could no longer be made. In an earlier age, had Windsor Castle been damaged by fire, there would have been no controversy at all about who paid for repairs to what is essentially the Queen's private residence. The taxpayer would have picked up the bill. However, on this occasion, once the Government had announced that it would pick up the bill, the taxpayers through their Members of Parliament, began to protest. In the end, the

Queen herself had to raise some money by charging tourists to look over Buckingham Palace.

Given all this, Fergie's debts and her habit of trading on her royal connections are nothing unique. And the belated acquiescence by the Queen that she should pay tax on her private income and contribute more to the upkeep of her own family has done little to correct an impression of the Windsors as both immensely rich and unwilling to pay their way. The Queen's decision to pay tax was seen as a cosmetic exercise. It did not convince the majority of people, those on pensions, fixed incomes, those who had to work hard and increasingly long hours in insecure jobs, that the gap between the immensely rich Windsors and themselves was in any way narrowing.

Yet, whatever its faults as a family, it still was a coherent family unit, or so people were led to believe during the sixties, seventies and eighties. In 1968, that most ardent of monarchists, almost spokesman for the family, Norman St John Stevas wrote in the *Spectator*: 'The example of a united family life set by the Queen and her consort is a real contribution to the nation's morality.'

However, Sarah Bradford's carefully worded pen picture of the marriage of the Queen and Prince Philip strongly suggests that romantic image suggested by Norman St John Stevas was, even when he wrote those words, far from realistic:

> The question of Philip's fidelity is, like the real extent of Elizabeth's personal fortune, the last bastion which courtiers will defend to the death. Money and sex, the two questions which most excite the public interest, are naturally the ones which the courtiers least want to see exposed. In defence of their Queen, even the most open and truthful of courtiers is prepared to lie or feign ignorance.
>
> Elizabeth notices; she is an exceptionally observant person. Once, at a party given in Scotland, Elizabeth was seated at a table beside the dance floor, ostensibly talking about racing. But her eyes were elsewhere and, as the dancers parted,

she could see her husband dancing very close to the hostess's daughter. She sees but she does not want to know, taking it all in her stride...

Theirs is a very royal marriage; Elizabeth's generation was not brought up to expect fidelity but loyalty. Philip is not the man to fall hopelessly in love. Elizabeth understands his desire for independence and to be his own man and makes allowances for it. Philip goes his own way, restless, always on the move. He makes his own plans, often without consulting his wife.

In the beginning the marriage was a success on every level; physically mentally and temperamentally the couple were compatible. Elizabeth was physically passionate and very much in love with her husband. Philip found her sexually attractive and was equally, although perhaps more coolly, in love. And importantly, for a man like Philip, he loved and respected her. Theirs was a traditional marriage. Elizabeth was used to a household in which the man came first and Philip was a particularly dominant male.

Only today have the rumours of Prince Philip's alleged extra-marital flings been aired, and other personal details, once hushed up, of the Windsor family life have been admitted to. It has been said publicly, for instance, that Princess Margaret attempted to commit suicide, even though Palace officials at the time lied to the people who were expecting to meet her, saying that she had a heavy cold and was therefore indisposed. It is now common knowledge, after many denials, that both the Prince and Princess of Wales committed adultery. In modern Britain, that a family has its weaknesses would be understood. There would be a degree of sympathy. What sticks in the throat of many in Britain is that while the royal family had its problems, it still expected to be seen as the model Christian family for the nation and lied over and over again to preserve that false image. Scandals, such as the birth of an illegitimate child to a former Prince of Wales in Australia, took seventy years to emerge.

The *annus horribilis* when it all came to a head was 1992. The long-time campaigner for the disestablishment of the Church of England, Bishop Colin Buchanan, described the effect of that year like this.

In the spring, Andrew Morton published his book, *Diana: Her True Story*, suggesting that the Prince of Wales had been a woodenly uncomprehending husband to a wife who could not cope with the pressures on her – and that she had succumbed not only to bulimia, but also to at least one attempt at suicide. Every incentive was given to the great British public to believe that the Princess of Wales had personally sanctioned the account. The Princess Royal quietly got a divorce from Mark Phillips, and in the autumn married again, in Scotland. No great shaking of thrones in that – probably most of us just wished her well. But during the summer the Duke and Duchess of York had also separated – and the Duchess had some fairly compromising, or at least suggestive, photos of her taken by zoom lens during a holiday when she was with her American financial adviser. Then came the transcribing and replaying of a telephone call between the Prince of Wales and one Camilla P.-B. This went a long way to suggest a sustained guilty relationship between the two of them, perhaps stretching quite some way into the past. Then the Prince and Princess of Wales formally separated, too – and by November 1992, they appeared irreconcilable.

At this point I encountered suddenly a complete mood-change in both press and public, and it is my belief that this was not merely a subjective personal impression but reflected an actual shift in the nation's outlook...Until mid-November 1992, whenever I got involved in discussions or disputes (formal or informal) about disestablishment, I knew that I could be as confrontational as I wished with most present features of the links between Church and State, but that the Queen's position was not only inviolable, but even unquestionable. If the logic of any change in, say, Prime Ministerial appointments, was that the Queen was to cease as Supreme Governor, then there was almost total market resistance to the notion. If a change would not touch the Crown – it could be looked at. But if it would touch the Crown – then it was virtual treason to propose it, and only the imbecilic or b-minded or bomb-throwing anarchist could persevere with it...

But overnight this changed. Suddenly I began to get calls from the daily tabloids and even the quality Sundays, and occasionally the radio and television, and the questions now all took the same form: 'Do not the troubles of the Palace, and particularly of the Prince of Wales, mean that the Church of England will have to be disestablished?' The Palace, which had had a thicket-fence round it until that mid-November, and was thus impenetrable for disestablish-mentarians, had suddenly exposed a *weakness* within the thicket-fence; and Palace-watchers, instead of protecting the Crown in its establishment role, were themselves asking whether, as a matter of public confidence, the Crown could sustain the responsibility which the Supreme Governorship of the Church of England placed upon it. And it has to be said that the fascination of that question has run on and on, and fifteen months later shows little sign of abating. I was in the studio audience of a Sky TV production in February 1993, and George Austin, the Archdeacon of York, who was a protagonist in the discussion, said words to this effect: 'I have never agreed with Colin Buchanan on establishment issues, but I find now that the prospect of having a man who has cheated on his wife since soon after they were married as Supreme Governor of the Church of England fills me with alarm.'

It was not just traditional clerics who were beginning to ask the questions which previously had been the exclusive territory of dangerous republicans. Many elderly people who had cheered the young Queen back in 1953 and been ardent monarchists all their lives were becoming increasingly shocked, hurt and disillusioned. They felt badly let down, betrayed by a story they had believed in. When the Queen Mother dies, and she is now well into her nineties, the older generation in Britain will lose their last link with the old days when loyalty to the royal family and respect for it as an institution were taken for granted.

It could, of course, be argued that the House of Windsor cannot be in that bad odour, as people still flock by their thousands to Garden Parties and eagerly hope to be included on the New Year and Birthday Honours' List. But the question that needs to be asked is, which is most important to these people, a sign of public recognition or the chance to meet a member of the Windsor family? One suspects that it is the former. Few people turn down an invitation to the Scottish Garden Party at Holyrood held by the Queen's High Commissioner, when there is no member of the House of Windsor in sight. One would also suspect that should the House of Windsor be replaced by another dynasty, being presented to a new monarch would carry the same kudos.

Apologists for the House of Windsor are reduced to one line of defence. They acknowledge all the failings of the royal family, their wealth, their privilege and their marital problems but always add 'but I wouldn't say a word against the Queen – she is doing a magnificent job'. For them, that phrase has become their mantra.

And yet, curiously, if it was a large company or even a Government that was at present falling in disarray, there would be no hesitation in laying the blame at the door of the person at the top. A constitutional monarch has two roles: one is to unobtrusively perform the functions of Head of State in a manner which gains the general approval of the people, and the other is to provide an heir suitable and ready to take over the position. In the first regard, after 44 years of experience, it is highly regrettable that the Queen is still capable of making extraordinarily insensitive mistakes. She does not make the grossly politically incorrect statements attributed to her husband – like the one he made on an official visit to China about people with 'slitty eyes'. Yet, on her visit to Poland early in 1996, her oversight and negligence fully warranted the *Guardian* headline 'Gaffe mars Queen's visit'.

Royal officials were forced to admit another embarrassing blunder when the Queen delivered the wrong speech to the Polish parliament yesterday and omitted a crucial paragraph commemorating the suffering of the Polish Jews in the Second World War.

The visit is increasingly being seen as accident-prone after last-minute alterations had to be made to the Queen's itinerary last week following criticism from prominent British Jews that she would not be laying a wreath at Auschwitz in memory of Holocaust victims.

The Queen failed to include in her keynote address: 'Nor can we ever forget the suffering of the Polish people under Nazi occupation, nor the terrible fate of the Polish Jews'.

A Buckingham Palace spokesman said last night that the omission was 'entirely unintentional' and due to a 'typographical error' which had not been properly checked. 'It was purely a mistake, for which the Queen's advisers take full responsibility.'

On Monday, the Queen visited the Umschlagplatz Jewish memorial in Warsaw for a hastily arranged wreath-laying ceremony in memory of Holocaust victims, after talks between Buckingham Palace and the Foreign Office on Friday.

Yesterday's slip will fuel disappointment that, unlike most visiting heads of state, the Queen did not visit Auschwitz. The Board of Deputies of British Jews had expressed its disappointment. The Queen is to visit Krakow today, only 40 minutes away, but Buckingham Palace insisted the schedule is very tight.

It must be hoped the Queen is competent behind the scenes. The Queen meets the Prime Minister and should, over the years, have accumulated a certain wisdom to advise. But essentially, to be a successful monarch, the day-to-day public job has to be performed well, and an heir has to be provided.

By these yard sticks Queen Elizabeth II has been a failure. On the family front, perhaps the inability of her children to create stable family lives of their own relates back to their mother. The Queen's biographer Sarah Bradford wrote: '"Motherhood is not the Queen's strong suit," a friend said. "She likes getting on with her job and she is extremely busy."' Even in the early years of her reign, she only kept an hour for the children in the morning and another for bath-time, but otherwise saw no harm in their spending most of their time in the company of nannies and governesses.

And a very telling detail of how little has changed emerges from Sarah Bradford's biography when she writes of the Queen's relationship with her two daughters-in-law, or at least, how it was before the family break-ups.

> If Diana and Sarah had wanted something they would simply go over the Heads of the Household and wheedle: 'Oh, Ma'am, please, just this once...the Household hate me.'

What sort of family can it be where a mother is so conscious of her dignity and status that even her daughters-in-law have to address her in her formal style of 'Ma'am'?

In an article in the *Observer* to mark the Queen's seventieth birthday in 1996, Andrew Rawnsley was brutal in his assessment of the Queen's achievements.

> Fish stink from the head. Institutions rot from the top. That is the rule we apply to all other walks of public life. The captain carries the can when confidence collapses in the Conservative Party or the England football team or British Gas.

Why should this leader expect or receive different treatment because she wears a tiara?

The Queen calls her family business 'The Firm'. So let us consider her record as chief executive of British Monarch, monopoly suppliers of nationhood and pageantry. The balance sheet is stained with red. Huge reserves of consumer goodwill have been dissipated. Attempts to rebrand the product have only accelerated the decline in market share to the point where the organisation has lost so much of its customer base that even its remaining supporters widely expect it to go into liquidation.

The collapse of The Firm during her reign as chief executive is the more astonishing considering the impregnability of the position she inherited.

All the hopes and expectations of the new Elizabethan age portrayed in all the sycophantic and sugary language written and uttered at the time of the coronation in 1953 have gone. Whatever Queen Elizabeth II is like in private, to her public she is an austere middle-aged to elderly woman with a silly, squeaky, upper-class voice, with no warmth, devoid of all public emotion, who likes horses and corgis, assumes she has an unquestioned right to live in four different magnificent palaces and to be addressed as 'Your Majesty' or 'Ma'am'. In providing an heir, indeed a happy family, she and her irritable husband have failed, as she has also failed to understand her people. The most telling extract from a recent documentary about the Queen was one in which she was meeting a group of pensioners over a cup of tea. She could have been a Martian. She was so alien to that environment. She had no small talk, no point of contact, and, it appeared, little empathy.

Sarah Bradford, speaking to Valerie Grove in *The Times* in January 1996, tried to put something of a favourable spin onto Queen Elizabeth's idiosyncrasies and failings.

The Queen inherited the dutiful, dignified mien of Queen Victoria, whose vow was 'I will be good'. Even as a small child she was disciplined, punctual and orderly. When she was two, Churchill noted, 'She has an air of authority and reflectiveness astonishing in an infant.' She also inherited the 'canine' looks (Bradford's apposite word) of her grandmother, Mary of Teck.

It was Queen Mary who decreed that royal ladies should not smile. 'Too awful! Smiling!' she would comment if a regal smile were captured on camera. Hence her own severe mask. 'I think the Queen Mother changed all that. She has a smiling sort of face, while the Queen, on some days, seems to be fixed in her Miss Piggy mode.'

In the same article, Valerie Grove wrote:

Rebecca West said that the monarchy is 'a presentation of ourselves behaving well' but, as Ms Bradford says, when the Queen tried to preserve some kind of 'normal' life for her children, they began to behave just like their contemporaries, and in some ways worse. So the overall picture of royal family life is not edifying: outsiders in the family get severely tested or frozen out. There is, Ms Bradford says, a naïvety about the family's socializing: they end up making terrible connections with appalling people, 'blinkered gentry living in Hampshire' – that's their reality. They make marriages out of propinquity. You only have to live next to them in Norfolk. Nothing propinks like propinquity, as P. G. Wodehouse says.

The smallness of the royal circle of friends is very striking. They have to get others to draw up lists of suitable people to be invited to their bigger parties. The Queen Mother is rather different: she takes her own initiative, she wasn't brought up royal, she's like a social lady of her time and class, which the Queen is not.

Gathered in one volume, the remorseless stream of family disasters in recent years, the galloping divorces, the taped telephone conversations with lovers – 'what Julian Barnes called "the sexual and marital tomfoolery of the Queen's whelps"' – the scandals surrounding embarrassing new in-laws such as Major Ronald Ferguson, the rumblings over paying taxes, the horrors of IRA madmen creating mayhem, such things might overwhelm a lesser woman. And it would not have happened to a more upright person. But Her Majesty stands aloof from it all, a still, small, imperturbable voice, carrying on. Only in her *annus horribilis* speech, delivered with a heavy cold, did she come near to expressing dismay...

'She innately knows how to do the job. She does not court popularity. She does her duty. She is fascinated by people outside, and wants to know what's going on, but doesn't think of herself as "winning hearts". That's not her thing.'

Regrettably, and this is a most damning thing to say about the Queen, she actually appears to believe that she is different and important. She seems to think she deserves respect and sub-servience because of who she is, and appears not to believe that she has to deserve and earn that respect. She is so used to being whisked around the world with the utmost efficiency, never carrying money, being lauded, praised and humoured at every move that she illustrates admirably that biblical admonition 'beware when all men praise you'. She might want to know 'what's going on outside', but she has no point of contact, no comprehension and therefore no empathy. She asked to see what it was like in a court of law but was prevented by obscure tradition, from visiting unobtrusively, and so an entire court scene had to be reconstruct-ed and play-acted for her benefit.

It was over 30 years ago that Lord Altrincham warned that this might happen when he pointed out that all the Queen's advisers came from a single strata of society. The Queen did not heed his warning. Britain is a multi-racial country. The Commonwealth much more so, yet the Queen's circle of advisers and courtiers is almost exclusively drawn from the white upper and upper middle classes.

It would be unfair, however, to blame the Queen entirely for her remoteness from her subjects. First of all, one has to blame the notion that she has subjects. She is not just a Head of State, a representative of the people, the people belong to her. To be a subject is a feudal notion, quite the opposite of being a citizen. But all her life the Queen has lived surrounded by privilege. Indeed, to smother a whole family with such privilege is a form of inhumanity. It is a gross intrusion into the life of a teenage boy that cameras are trained on him at school, as happens every day with Prince William. If there was one single argument for abolishing the monarchy that now exists in Britain it is that it is a form of cruelty to the family involved. No wonder Queen Elizabeth II has emerged from this luxurious, gilded torture chamber as such a cold fish, with an unchallenged idea of her own importance.

# 4

## *Route to a Republic*

We hold these truths to be self-evident, that all men are created equal, that they are endowed by their Creator with certain unalienable Rights, that among these are Life, Liberty and the pursuit of Happiness. – That to secure these rights, Governments are instituted among Men, deriving their just powers from the consent of the governed, – That whenever any Form of Government becomes destructive of these ends, it is the Right of the People to alter or to abolish it, and to institute new Government, laying its foundation on such principles and organizing its powers in such form, as to them shall seem most likely to effect their Safety and Happiness.

When, in 1776, the American colonists renounced King George III and became an independent state, they chose the republican model. An examination of the Declaration of Independence shows that they did not throw the monarchy aside lightly. Indeed the declaration stated that it was prudent not to change a long-established government for light and transient causes. Nevertheless, the original fathers of America felt that the time had come for the Hanoverian monarch sitting on a throne some three thousand miles away to be replaced. Accordingly, a new constitution was constructed with great care and George Washington became the first President of the United States of America. The rest, as they say, is history.

The American model of government has had both its successes and failures. It has produced some outstanding presidents and some enlightened governments. It has also succeeded in placing certain utter rogues in the White House and the Constitution was unable to prevent a fierce and bloody civil war in the last century.

Perhaps many people in Britain owe an aversion to the presidential system to what they see across the Atlantic in America. Many people in Britain find it hard to square in their minds the idea that the person to whom all deference should be shown as Head of State is the same person who over the preceding years has fought, bribed and lied his way to the top, by which time his personal life and finances have been ruthlessly dissected by the press. Suddenly, the vilified rogue of the election campaign to whom, at most current elections, fewer than 30 per cent of the voting population have given their support, suddenly becomes the person who embodies the State and to whom all honour must be shown. Many British people feel more comfortable that the Prime Minister, the career politician, has his or her place in the bear pit of parliament, while the Queen remains gloriously detached from politics.

The presidential system, however, does not have to follow the American pattern. In Ireland, the president is non-executive and the holder of the office remains above day-to-day party politics. When in the hands of someone of the stature and perception of Mary Robinson, it is an institution which commands a great deal of popularity and affection. Similarly in Iceland, where the president, who retires after sixteen years in office, is held in such high regard that she has been re-elected to her non political post with 90 per cent of the popular vote. On the other hand, as has been seen in Austria, a titular state president with Nazi skeletons in his cupboard can become an embarrassment to the entire State.

To political theorists, a president and a monarch can either be at opposite ends of the political spectrum or two versions of the same thing. A monarch is literally a single ruler – as is a president in many countries where the absolute ruler or dictator is frequently styled 'The President'. In that instance the two rulers, however styled, might be one and the same thing. Indeed the tyrannical President Bokassa of the Central African Republic, modelling himself on his hero Napoleon, had himself crowned Emperor and his country declared an Empire.

Elected presidents, under most democratic constitutions, are subject to checks and balances – hence the recent lengthy power struggle between the US Congress and President Clinton over the federal budget. Where monarchs and presidents are said to be found at opposite ends of the political spectrum it is where a president is elected and only operates as one of a constitutional team, and the monarch is not elected. And what of the presidents who are elected and then have absolute power? They are not dissimilar to monarchs like the Pope, except that normally some mechanism exists to remove a tired, incapacitated or discredited president. Even President Hastings Banda was in the end removed, although it must be acknowledged that such over-powering presidents are not normally removed except by the military.

Given all these variations in definition of monarch and president it is not surprising that many people are naturally puzzled by the idea that a monarch can exist in, or in some way be compatible with, a democracy. Take this telling interchange from Peter van Greenaway's *The Man who Held the Queen to Ransom and Sent Parliament Packing*:

'A democratic monarchy is as impossible as a pyramid balancing on its summit.'

'Then why does it exist sir?'

'Why? Well, Private Kemp, someone once said, "It exists because no one quite knows what to do with it".'

For Britain to opt for the republican system would be a huge wrench. First of all it would require a change in the name of the country. It would no longer be the United Kingdom of Great Britain and Northern Ireland but perhaps the People's Republic of Great Britain and Northern Ireland. Indeed, if Scotland was to go its own way and Northern Ireland be given a new status, then that which remained of the country might in future be known as the People's Republic of England and Wales. There would be a huge legislative upheaval involved in setting up a republic, as every institution of government would have to be altered. Of course there are precedents, and when former member states of the British Empire became independent, those that did not retain the Queen as Head of State went through that mammoth and daunting process of change. For many of these countries, of course, they were merely throwing off a system of government which had only been in place for a few decades, perhaps a century at the most. In Britain the upheaval would be enormous because the current system of government can be traced back at least 900 years.

What would the consequences be? Would all the pageantry of British life be lost? Would the Yeomen of the Guard re-dedicate themselves to serve a president in a lounge suit? Would the Changing of the Guard continue? How much in foreign earnings might be lost? Would tourists flock to the Tower of London and to Buckingham Palace if they were simply museums and had no claim to be part of a living heritage?

It was when Queen Victoria, following a long period in which she had been out of the public eye – during which she still expected parliament and the taxpayers to finance her lifestyle and that of her extensive family – that republicanism was last fashionable in Britain. Today, Tony Benn, the Labour MP who renounced his peerage to sit in the House of Commons, is the successor to that lobby of Victorian Members of Parliament who were then the republican standard bearers. This is the preamble to Tony Benn's Bill to Abolish the Monarchy.

A bill to establish a democratic, federal and secular Commonwealth of England, Scotland and Wales dedicated to the welfare of all its citizens; to establish fundamental human rights within that Commonwealth; to lower the voting age to 16 years and to make other provision with respect to elections, including equal representation for women; to prescribe a constitutional oath; to establish a Commonwealth Parliament consisting of the House of Commons and the House of the People and to make provision for the term of a Parliament and for legislative and other procedure; to establish the office of President, and a Council of State, and to prescribe the powers of each; to provide for the formation of governments; to amend the law relating to official information, the armed forces and the security services; to make fresh provision for the participation of Britain in the United Nations Organization and the European Communities and European Union; to make the basing of foreign forces in Britain dependent upon the approval of the House of Commons; to make new provision with respect to the judicial system and to establish a National Legal Service; to set up national Parliaments for England, Scotland and Wales; to amend the law relating to local government, the district auditor and the accountability of police forces; to end the constitutional status of the Crown and to make certain consequential provision; to abolish the House of Lords and the Privy Council, to end the recognition in law of personal titles, and to provide for the acknowledgement of service to the community; to disestablish the Church of England, abolish the offence of blasphemy, and to provide for equality under the law for all religions and beliefs; to end British jurisdiction in Northern Ireland; to provide for constitutional amendment; and to make transitional and related provision.

Tony Benn presented his bill in 1991, a little ahead of the present renewed interest in republicanism, or rather hostility to the Windsors. It attracted a certain modest interest, but little support from outside his own group of followers. Although a Privy Counsellor and an ex-minister, Mr Benn is not of the political establishment.

His bill did not set off a ground swell of popular support either inside or outside parliament. The reason for this is possibly twofold. First of all, he was a little ahead of his time, and in the second instance, he did not strike quite the right note. It all sounded very seventeenth century, harking back to the days of Cromwell's talk of Commonwealth and the radicals of that bygone era, the Levellers and the Diggers. This is perhaps not surprising as Tony Benn himself is a great admirer of those two groups of pioneer socialists. Again, to include within the bill changes to the voting age and the abolition of titles was perhaps too all-embracing. And the section of the bill dealing with an elected president was so grey and clinical that there was little chance that any of the residual magic of monarchy and nation would survive.

> THE PRESIDENT: There shall be a President elected from amongst their number, by a two-thirds majority, by both Houses of Parliament sitting together, to serve for a three-year term and to be eligible for re-election for one further three-year term.

There was not even to be a popular election for the president, no chance of the true 'people's choice' emerging from outside the existing narrow confines of political life. So, right from the start, the constituency from which the new president could be chosen was to be restricted by Benn to some one thousand people, almost all of whom had been or were still subject to the control and patronage of the party machines. Thus if the grassroots preference was for one of the old royals, Princess Anne perhaps, or one of the new meritocracy, say Richard Branson, or a celebrated writer, artist or musician, that person would be ineligible to stand for election under the Benn plan. His whole notion smacked too much of jobs for the boys or girls.

Furthermore, even if the man or woman chosen as president was acceptable to the wider electorate, Benn suggested a curious hotchpotch of powers.

(a) The powers now exercised under Crown Prerogative shall be exercised by the President, who shall act solely upon the advice of the Prime Minister, or of a resolution of the House of Commons (which shall prevail if such resolution is in conflict with the advice of the Prime Minister);

(b) the exercise of such powers shall require the assent of the House of Commons before having effect; and

(c) the powers of the President shall include power –
  – to give assent to the passage of legislation;
  – to dissolve Parliament;
  – to invite a person to attempt to form an administration;
  – to make orders for any purpose for which Orders in Council were required before the coming into force of this Act;
  – to declare war;
  – to order British forces into armed conflict;
  – to make peace;
  – to recognise foreign governments;
  – to sign or ratify treaties;
  – to grant pardons;
  – to grant charters;
  – to make appointments;
  – to establish commissions of inquiry;
  – to grant commissions in the armed forces;
  – to issue orders; and
  – to exercise other executive powers not conferred by statute.

It must seriously be asked why the powers under clause (c) need be there. Are they not just throwbacks to the days of the monarchy? Legislation can surely come into force once it has gone through all its parliamentary stages. The need for the assent to be given only continues the pretence that all political power was exercised through the monarch. As to Orders in Council, are these not today used by the executive as a way of bypassing parliament? Laws are enacted by this anachronistic procedure to save the executive time, to enable it to squeeze laws through by a back-door method, in order to avoid having its plans and policies scrutinized in the committee rooms of the House of Commons. Is Tony Benn really suggesting the continuation of this current and common abuse by the executive of the democratic system? Indeed, he is giving a new twist to it, for he proposes to replace an apolitical monarch with a political president who has possibly been nominated by the executive for the post and been elected with the help of the party whips.

And when it comes to the president having such absolute authority over the armed forces, if he or she is a former active politician with cunning and ambition, the danger exists that a president might decide to exercise that power. Imagine the scenario of the two chambers of the reformed parliament deciding to let bygones be bygones and elect a distinguished former Prime Minister as President. Lady Thatcher is sworn in. The Argentines invade the Falklands again. Her Prime Minister advises that Britain settle diplomatically. The President decides otherwise.

Surely one of the aims of any constitutional reform should be the ending of such absolute power, a power which after all only exists in the case of the Queen as a hangover from a former age.

Then comes a section in the bill dealing with the constitutional status of the Crown. This would be undoubtedly necessary to enact the whole, but some people might admit to certain qualms. There is no sense of continuity allowed for, no gradual changeover from the familiar to the unfamiliar. It is an abrupt change, and Britain is a country with a sense of history. It is a very bald and final statement.

> The legal status of the Crown is hereby ended and the Monarch for the time being, and his or her heirs and successors, shall cease to enjoy, or exercise as Monarch, any political or personal power of any kind, either directly through the person of the Monarch, or by prerogative, or through Ministers.

The new, reformed Britain needs to derive some authority from its past or the new constitution will in some deep-seated and uneasy way feel illegal or improper.

Then comes the matter of crown property and compensation. At least if the deed is to be done, Tony Benn is fair. There are to be no beheadings on the scaffold or public humiliation of the ex-royals. They are not to be sent to live in a council house.

> The ownership and control of all Crown lands, buildings and property which are held by the Monarch for the time being, as a consequence of his or her occupancy of the Throne, or their position as heirs to the Throne, shall be transferred forthwith to the Commonwealth Government.
>
> Compensation:
> (1) A payment shall be paid from public funds to the person occupying the Throne at the coming into force of this Act, to dispose of as he or she thinks fit.
> (2) A pension shall be paid to the person occupying the Throne at the moment of coming into force of this Act.
> (3) Accommodation shall be made available for such members of the former Royal family, in such Royal Palaces as shall be determined by Parliament.

And inevitably, once the ex-royals become ordinary citizens, they become liable to pay taxes.

> All members of the Royal Family shall be liable for the payment of taxes and charges paid by a citizen of the Commonwealth, or a person residing in the Commonwealth, as the case may be.

No cause for complaint there, but Tony Benn does not stop at the abolition of the monarchy.

The House of Lords is hereby abolished, and from the coming into force of this Act no person shall enjoy any legal status as a Lord Spiritual or Temporal, and any person who was formerly a member of the House of Lords shall enjoy the right to stand for Parliament.

At that point one trusts, should the bill be debated and Tony Benn is still sitting on the Commons' green benches, he will rise to his feet and declare a personal interest.

Few can quarrel with the next clause – 'The Privy Council, and the style and precedence of Privy Counsellor, are hereby abolished' – yet what is to be gained by the abolition if a Council of State replaces it?

Then comes that part of the bill which will cause considerable distress to all knights of the shires, baronets, minor peers, sons of dukes and earls, holders of the OBE and many hundreds if not thousands of others.

(1) No personal title or rank, whether hereditary or not, shall be recognised in law.

(2) No personal title, rank or dignity shall be conferred, nor shall any admission be made to a rank or class of an order of chivalry or any similar order.

(3) The Commonwealth Parliament and the national Parliaments may express gratitude to those citizens who have distinguished themselves through service to the community by Resolutions of Thanks.

One senses various Benn bees from the Old Labour bonnet buzzing away. Are not titles and honours a harmless bit of fun? That hereditary peers should have a vote in parliament and that corporate givers to Conservative party funds should be knighted is indefensible, but that the charity worker who has given selfless and lifelong service to a good cause should not wear his or her

MBE is perhaps going a bit too far. Far more relevant a change to the constitution is the bill's declaration of rights.

(1) All citizens of Britain shall be entitled to enjoy, and to campaign for, universal, democratic and enforceable rights, both individual and collective, enshrined in law, adhered to in practice and respected by society, as a precondition of self-government and the achievement of full political, social and economic emancipation within a civilised society:

(2) Every citizen shall have the following political rights:
– to freedom of speech;
– to freedom of assembly and of association for the purpose of expressing an opinion, without interference from the State;
– to organize for common political, social or economic ends;
– to practise, or not to practise, any or all religions;
– to vote in all elections, participate in all electoral processes and institutions, and to contest all elections;
– to privacy and the protection of personal information and correspondence from surveillance or interference;
– to information about public, political, social or economic affairs;
– to freedom of movement, unhindered by arbitrary interference, and to be given asylum from political, social or economic oppression; and
– to conscientious objection to service in the armed forces.

(3) Every citizen shall have the following legal rights:
– to personal freedom from arbitrary arrest, detention or harassment;
– to a fair and impartial hearing by a jury of the citizen's peers if accused of any unlawful activity; and to equal treatment before the law and equal access to legal representation;

– to be presumed innocent until proved guilty, to be informed of all charges laid and the evidence in support of them, and the right to silence in court;

– to freedom from torture or cruel and degrading treatment, and from capital punishment;

– to legal advice and services, free at the point of use; and

– to equal treatment before the law, and in the community, without discrimination, and regardless of race, sex or sexual preference, colour, religious or political conviction or disability.

(4) Every citizen shall have the following social rights:

– to adequate and warm housing and comfortable living conditions;

– to rest, recreation and leisure, to a limitation of working hours and to holidays;

– to enjoy access to literature, music, the arts and cultural activities;

– to good health care and preventive medicine, free at the moment of need;

– to lifelong and free educational provision;

– to dignity and care in retirement;

– in the case of women, to control of their own fertility and reproduction;

– to free and equal access to child care;

– to free, effective and equitable means of transportation;

– to a healthy, sustainable, accessible and attractive environment and to clean water and air;

– to media free from governmental or commercial domination; and

– to full access to personal information held by any public authority, subject only to a restriction order signed by a Minister and reported to Parliament.

(5) Every citizen shall have the following economic rights:

– to useful work at a fair wage that provides an income sufficient to maintain a decent standard of living;

– to belong to a trade union and to withdraw labour in pursuit of an industrial dispute;
– to participate in all decisions, including those relating to health and safety, affecting the workplace, and to information, representation and expression of opinion for all employed persons;
– to full and equal access to all state or social benefits at a level sufficient to meet basic needs; and
– to freedom from taxation in excess of an ability to pay.

Give or take debate over the details, a British declaration of rights is long overdue. The question that must be asked is this: cannot a bill of Rights be introduced far more simply without it being linked in with the republican cause? Is there not a danger that the rights might be lost because the wholesale political revolution is unacceptable?

To round off this review of the Benn bill, let us look at the Oath which Benn proposes be made in the following terms, and shall be declared in the presence of another person who has taken the Oath, who shall report the names of all those who have taken the Oath before him or her to the President. Why Benn feels a nation in his brave new republican world needs the ritual mumbo jumbo of oath-taking is not explained in the bill. What is clear from the Oath however is that God has been taken right out of it.

I...do solemnly declare and affirm that I will be faithful to the Constitution of the Commonwealth of Britain, and will respect its laws, as enacted by Parliament; will preserve inviolably the civil rights and liberties of the people, including the right to self-government, through their elected representatives, and will faithfully and truly declare my mind and opinion on all matters that come before me without fear or favour.

The Benn approach, flawed in its details as it might be, is certainly a utilitarian option. It would no doubt be functional, but probably be little loved. Arguably, it was the austerity of the Cromwellian experiment which finally resulted in its demise and the return of King Charles II at the Restoration. It was the time when maypoles were abolished and Christmas festivities frowned upon. One suspects that the Benn bill comes from the same puritan, killjoy stable. There needs to be some fun in life, even political life, and the great strength in having a constitutional monarchy is that it can provide colour as well as political continuity.

There also needs to be mystery. And what has been allowed to happen under the Windsors is that the spiritual mystery underpinning the monarchy of old has vanished.

Yet, in an age of confusion, secularization, pantheism and fundamentalism, there is still perhaps a glimmer of hope that somehow something of the mystery can be revived. Unless it is through Princess Diana, it is highly unlikely that any member of the House of Windsor can rekindle this element of mystery, but unless it is rekindled, something of the soul of the nation will be irrevocably lost. There is no way of defining this, but something in the collective mind of the British people still yearns for a symbol to suggest to them that there is something more to their society than simply a disparate and unconnected collection of just over 55 million individuals. National identity, once thought to have been a dying notion, is making a comeback. Artificial unions of states into political conglomerates are breaking up – the old Soviet Union is a prime example. In Britain, people have been persistently told by the right-wing thinkers that market forces shape economic destinies and that the most important values lie in economic success and competitiveness rather than in morality or ethics. Lady Thatcher famously said there was no such thing as society. And yet, many would argue that national identities do exist in a set of common experiences, values, customs and assumptions. If this is the case, the British identity is made up of more than self-interest. It includes a shared concept of monarchy, a residual folk-faith, a set of familiar institutions. There is much grumbling that goes on but anyone who dares remove red telephone boxes from the street corners or change policemen's helmets to flat caps is asking for a heap of trouble. And these are just the trivial details of Britishness.

And it is within this context of national identity, where certain things can be said to be held to be sacrosanct, that the objection to a possible change-over from a monarch to a president must be seen. For it is a total challenge to the self-image of a people and could be a source of much insecurity and anger. Tony Benn's bill, as logical and democratic as it is in the main, goes far too far. Reform the House of Lords, yes, but abolish it? In its anachronistic way, the traditional scarlet and gold upper chamber serves a very useful and civilized purpose. No other country has devised a better way of getting rid of troublesome has-been politicians. They queue up for 'promotion'. Dress them in ermine and they are willing to be politically neutered. Even Lady Thatcher knows she can never make a come-back from the House of Lords.

One of the very few radical proposals suggested by the New Labour leader Tony Blair with which his parliamentary colleague Tony Benn would agree, is that the hereditary peers should be deprived of their parliamentary privileges. Yet it is interesting to note how many people are prepared to defend the House of Lords as it is now constituted. Andrew Roberts, writing in the Sunday Times in February 1996 claimed,

> ...paradoxically the House of Lords is not as unpopular as Blair's house. Largely free from sleaze, its members are not despised like today's MPs. As Gilbert and Sullivan put it in *The Pirates of Penzance*: 'No Englishman unmoved that statement hears, Because with all our faults we love our House of Peers'.

Roberts drew on Bagehot to make a further timeless and undated point. The Victorian constitutionalist had defended the order of nobility not on the grounds of its usefulness or creativity but on the grounds of what it prevented. 'It prevents the rule of wealth and the religion of gold.' Roberts goes on,

Rather than encouraging classlessness, as Blair intends, it is likely that his reforms will merely lessen the attraction of entering the House of Lords for ambitious and talented people. They will console themselves with simply amassing money instead.

Stripped of its historic grandeur by association and its unique human contact with the greatest days of the nation's past, ordinary Britons will surely lose their desire to enter the place. If the only people there are other political appointees, who owe their seats to political toadyism, what splendour attaches to membership? Surely, the hereditary peers can safely be left in place – but deprived of their attendance allowances and with the Commons given the right to discount the votes of any hereditary peers should any matter voted upon in the Lords contradict the will of the Lower House.

So when examining how the House of Windsor might be replaced, and what constitutional reforms could accompany the change, it might be as well not to present an option which is so alien and threatening that it will be opposed and shunned leaving the Windsors *in situ* for another century.

'There is much to be said for the British device of presenting a façade of a mystic monarchy, surrounded by bearskins, dukes and Gold Sticks, behind which the real machinery of government can function quietly and unnoticed.' So said Anthony Sampson in his *Anatomy of Britain Today*, some thirty years before the Royal House of Windsor had contributed to its demise by undermining that façade of mystery. There is much to be said now for the restoration of a new, more acceptable façade with which the British people might again feel comfortable. How might this be accomplished? There are a number of possible ways, and the first to be examined is that which involves the least constitutional upheaval: the abolition of primogeniture.

# 5

## *The First Born*

Primogeniture is the principle by which the first-born son of a monarch succeeds on the death of his father or mother. In the event of there being no son, a daughter may inherit the throne. Where no legitimate children are available, the succession goes to the king's eldest brother, or, should a Queen be on the throne, to the Queen's sister. The underlying principles of primogeniture are that men have precedence over women and the elder over the younger.

It is taken for granted that this is the system by which Queen Elizabeth II's heir is chosen. Prince Charles will become king and, unlike her childless namesake of four hundred years before, this Queen has a whole queue of family members in line should anything disastrous happen to the Prince of Wales. Primogeniture is a well-tried and tested procedure, say the monarchists; it is a dicey genetic lottery, say its opponents.

Primogeniture is assumed to be so firmly rooted in historical precedent that it is unchangeable. Yet, the single English (or rather, Saxon) king to have earned himself the title of 'the Great' was not a product of this system of inheritance. He was the younger brother of his predecessor Aethelred and the fifth son of King Aethelwulf. He undoubtedly came of royal stock but was declared King Alfred on merit.

Although a supporter, on balance, of the current practice, Harold Nicolson tells in his book *Monarchy* how primogeniture has not always been practised in these islands.

In Anglo-Saxon times the leader of the tribes, who from 829 became known as the 'Bretwalda' or 'king of the English', was elected by the Witan from members of the royal family. They generally chose for that purpose, among the older males of the family, the one whom they regarded as the most competent. When William the Conqueror established his dynasty the principle was, at least in theory, maintained that the king should be 'recognized' by the *Commune Concilium*, the successor of the Anglo-Saxon Witan. In practice, however, the Normans enforced, whenever they were able to do so, the principle of primogeniture under which the sovereign was automatically succeeded by his eldest son.

This system has certain obvious advantages. On the death of a sovereign, his heir ascends the throne immediately and can claim immediate allegiance. *Le roi est mort. Vive le roi.* The competition of rival claimants was thereby eliminated and in most cases no dynastic or civil wars ensued. Moreover, the accepted heir could be educated from childhood in the task of kingship and would not, when he inherited his responsibilities, be wholly untrained: tradition and continuity would be preserved.

A hereditary monarch, succeeding his father by primogeniture, had certain other advantages which are denied to an elected president or a dictator who seizes power by force. Being born in the purple, he has no political past, and as such has no party followers whom he is supposed to reward and no party antagonists who regard him with disfavour. He is not driven, as dictators are invariably driven, to win popular support by spectacular triumphs or to gain the obedience of the people by inventing some foreign menace. His aim is to personify stability rather than adventure, continuity rather than change. Representing as he does the nation as a whole, he should be in the position to mitigate class antagonism or partisan strife. If he be a man of wisdom and if he reign long enough to become a man of experience, he will come to be regarded as neutral in politics and as the embodiment of the national desire, character, and good sense.

The disadvantages of the hereditary principle are also apparent. It is at least unlikely that any royal family will provide a succession of intelligent and virtuous heirs. There are bound to occur monarchs whose judgement is unreliable, whose balance is uncertain, and whose understanding of the principles of parliamentary kingship is as shallow as their conception of the duty imposed on them in return for their high inheritance. There are bound to occur silly, irresponsible and even debauched kings. Yet under the system of strictly limited monarchy the damage that can be occasioned by such foolish or indulgent persons is also limited. In modern conditions the principle of primogeniture is certainly the best that can be adopted.

It is fortunate then, from Nicolson's point of view, that the heir does not have to prove his or her worth.

The pre-historic magic rites, which figured prominently in the coronation ceremonies of the Irish kings, were not adopted in the English *ordo*. In Ireland, the 'border line between kings and gods appears to have been obliterated'. On his accession the new Irish king was expected to break in wild horses; to ride between two blocks of stone which would only admit a passage for a legitimate sovereign; and to induce a sacred Palaeolithic stone to roar aloud in recognition.

Nowadays, such displays of primeval magic are only required symbolically. The king-warrior element is symbolized in the modern coronation by the great swords that are delivered to the new

King or Queen and carried naked before the Monarch in the processions. Menacing and splendid the swords flash as they move down the aisle, and among them is 'Curtana', the sword of Mercy, with its point stubbed and snapped.

In seeking alternatives to the present system of government in Britain without totally abolishing it and replacing it with a utilitarian republic, primogeniture is the first question that needs to be addressed. Why should it be the case that it is the first-born son of the reigning monarch, or, where one does not exist, the first-born daughter, who succeeds to the throne? There is surely no good reason. It happens because it is a Norman tradition. Examining the record of the present dynasty, it is a practice which has failed badly twice in little over a century.

Looking around the world, there are other models which can be adopted. In some royal families, on the death or abdication of a monarch, the oldest child succeeds, regardless of gender. This is the case in Denmark, where a change from primogeniture was approved by the nation at a referendum in 1953, thus allowing the nation to have a Queen for the first time. In certain other countries, all the qualified members of the monarch's family, in theory, have a claim to be considered for the throne. What has to be decided, and hopefully in as peaceful a manner as possible, is which descendant has the better claim. It need not be the eldest son. It might even be the youngest child or a grandchild.

There have been a wide variety of methods employed over the centuries in order to allow a dynasty to choose an heir in circumstances where the inheritance is not simply one of primogeniture. Today, there are several royal families using some of these other approaches. An example is to be found in Swaziland, now ruled over by King Maswati III. When a Swazi king dies, his heir is chosen using what Veronica Maclean, in her book *Crowned Heads*, describes as a most complicated method, 'and one that must cause as many problems as it solves'.

The lengthy process involves innumerable scrupulously performed ancient rights and strictly observed taboos. If they are not carried out, some kind of national disaster, it is thought, is bound to follow.

> While the future king is still a minor (the heir is always young and unmarried) the mother of the late king who had up until then been the Queen Mother becomes the Queen Regent and rules the country with the help of the late king's senior brother till the Crown Prince comes of age and is crowned, at which point his own mother the Ndlovukezi, begins joint rule with her son and the Queen Regent retires.
>
> The Swazi monarchy is a dual monarchy. The monarch is regarded as the Father, the Queen Mother as the Mother of the Nation, and between them there is an undefined but delicate balance of power, the mother by tradition exercising a gentle but moderating influence over the son.

How might a revision of the current system of inheritance in Britain work in practice? It would probably be unwise and unwelcome to embark on a system as complicated as that which elected King Maswati.

On the death of the Queen or on her abdication, Parliament could be given the duty of reviewing the qualifications of the existing members of the royal family. In practice, this would be a matter guided by the Prime Minister, and the Cabinet would no doubt have the first opportunity to discuss the matter and put recommendations to Parliament. Indeed, in order to continue with that legal fiction 'The king is dead, long live the king', the succession could be determined in advance. At any time during the monarch's life, the Cabinet could make a recommendation to Parliament and an heir apparent, rather like a vice-president, would stand by. The advantage to the members of the royal House would be considerable. First of all, the person chosen as heir apparent would be someone who has, having reached mature years, a certain experience of the world and coping with his or her status and position. It would take the burden of being heir to the throne off the shoulders of a young man or woman when too young or immature to cope. It would also mean that unsuitable elder children would be excluded from the start, and embarrassments such as the succession of King Edward VIII would be avoided. In the past, the royals had their own ways of coping with these problems, and it is strongly rumoured that the eldest son of Edward VII was 'done away with' because he was so unsuited to being king. It is a mystery as to whether the Duke of Clarence really did die from natural causes. One school of thought suggests he was 'humanely put down' – in other words, murdered. Perhaps, when sufficient time has passed, the truth will emerge. Whatever the truth, there seems to be universal agreement that it was a good thing that his life was foreshortened. It appears he had learning difficulties, curious and disconcerting personality traits, and that his younger brother, later George V, was a far better choice to sit on the throne.

Another strong argument for revising the system of primogeniture is that it would be an immense kindness to the heir. Not that first sons are often murdered, these days at least, but they are daily open to assassination by the media. By abolishing his automatic right to succeed his father, it could well be argued today that a great deal of the pressure would be taken off Prince William. He would be able to enjoy something nearer to an ordinary life. The photographers would not necessarily be encamped at Eton, waiting to catch him off guard and sell their photos to the tabloids, if he were only one of many possible heirs and his position would not be confirmed until he was well into his adult years.

Let us suppose the Cabinet and Parliament were entrusted with the job today of nominating an heir apparent. It could well be that Prince Charles would be chosen, but there would be no implication in this that his sons would unquestioningly take over. On the other hand, the Cabinet or Parliament might prefer Princess Anne, Prince Andrew or Prince Edward, or look to see whether someone like the Duke of Kent or the Duke of Gloucester might make a suitable, uncontroversial, non-political monarch. The great advantage of re-examining the system of primogeniture would be that there would be very little that would have to be altered in terms of the Constitution. The change over from one monarch to the next is a well-practised procedure. It has taken place five times already this century. Ending primogeniture would involve a minimum of constitutional change and disruption. At the same time, it would only bring about marginal change, yet the changes that it did bring about might be sufficient to restore the House of Windsor in public esteem. A person chosen who could deserve the respect of the nation and perhaps earn the affection of the people, could also, through his or her character, restore some of the spiritual base on which the monarchy rests. This in turn could indeed restore the fortunes of the royal House.

If this change was to take place it could well be the case that the 'heir select' would undertake to the Cabinet and Parliament to change the style of the monarchy, to live less ostentatiously or extravagantly and follow a model of monarchy which Parliament and Cabinet might deem to be more appropriate for the modern age. Such an undertaking might be made a requirement for selection.

It could also be that the 'heir select' would derive a new authority from the people by being selected by Parliament. It might even be proposed, in order to provide a new mandate for the monarch, that his or her name is confirmed by the people at a referendum. A government might take the opportunity of asking an additional question of the people at the time of voting: Should the new sovereign succeed on the death of Queen Elizabeth or on some predetermined date when the Queen would be obliged to retire?

Thus, when the new monarch is presented for coronation, the assent offered by those gathered and shouted out in sturdy unison would be real and not merely symbolic.

The benefits to a young first-born son of the abolition of primogeniture cannot be over-emphasized. The pressures to which Prince Charles was subjected as a schoolboy were, judging from the evidence of the royal biographers, simply uncivilized. First of all there was the bizarre selection of Gordonstoun by his father as a proper place to raise and educate a prince. It was a tough, uncompromising, cold shower and morning run regime in which bullying was rife. The Queen, it appears, according to Sarah Bradford, did not intervene.

Elizabeth loved Charles and he loved her. But he was in awe of her, and she was undemonstrative in her affection. One courtier remembered being in the room when Charles came to say goodnight to his mother as she was working on her papers. After he had kissed her good night, he was on his way out when Elizabeth said absentmindedly: 'Goodnight darling.' Charles stopped in his tracks and turned round, saying in a surprised voice: 'You called me darling!'

Philip, although perversely capable of great kindness, was by nature a bully and he bullied Charles, sometimes bringing tears to his eyes. Elizabeth never moved to protect her son, principally because she believed her husband to be right, and secondly because she believed that his masculinity gave him the right to have the principal say in his eldest son's upbringing.

Elizabeth is good with small children but not with adults. She is not a hugger or a communicator on a personal level. Out of consideration for her adored husband in his difficult position as consort, she over-compensated by allowing him free rein in the upbringing of his son.

So the pressures on Charles had started even earlier than his unfortunate Gordonstoun days. Even his prep school days were interrupted by the tabloids far more than those of his younger siblings. Some of the stories they and the foreign press told were pure invention, as Jonathan Dimbleby has argued:

There is no truth whatever in the story that Prince Charles sold his autograph at any time. There is also no truth whatever that he sold his composition book to a classmate. In the first place he is intelligent and old enough to realise how embarrassing this would turn out to be, and second he is only too conscious of the interest of the press in anything to do with himself and his family. The suggestion that his parents kept him so short of money that he has to find other means to raise it is also a complete invention...

The Queen's press secretary issued a statement declaring that it was 'highly regrettable that the private essay of a schoolboy should have been published at all in this way', an expression of dismay still enough to arrest any temptation that British editors might have had to test the Palace and the law by translating *Der Stern*'s disclosures for the benefit of their own readers. The American media was not similarly inhibited: fastening on a claim made by *Der Stern* that the Prince had sold his essays for thirty shillings because he was short of cash, a team of investigative journalists from *Time* magazine traced a number of the financial transactions apparently involved in the sale of the document to *Der Stern*, which had allegedly bought the first serial rights for £10,000.

A few years later when at Gordonstoun there was the famous cherry brandy incident, when it was emblazoned across all the papers, the heir to the throne had broken the law by consuming alcohol in a public bar. Dimbleby gives this account of the incident and of the double-standards of the tabloids' exploitation of it:

Hopelessly self-conscious and embarrassed by the attention, the Prince retreated, 'desperately trying to look for somewhere else to go'. Followed by Donald Green, he walked straight into the public bar. 'I thought *My God! What do I do?* I looked round and everybody was looking at me. And I thought, *I must have a drink – that's what you are supposed to do in a bar*. I went and sat down at the bar and the barman said, *What do you want to drink?* I thought that you had to have alcohol in a bar, so I said *Cherry brandy*.' At that moment, a journalist walked in and the 'cherry brandy' incident became headline news.

Fifteen months earlier, when Colville requested a little privacy for the royal schoolboy, the newspapers had readily assented, the *Daily Mail* editorializing: 'The Queen and Prince Philip have made it known publicly that they want the heir to the throne to get a perfectly normal upbringing, unmarred by the disturbing effects of too much publicity. We agree. It is not only the wish of his parents but also of the whole nation…it would be the summit of stupidity if this bold and sensible policy were undermined by sensation-mongering or oppressive public curiosity.'

Undoubtedly there will be numerous cherry brandy incidents manufactured or hyped up by the press to embarrass Prince William before he comes of age. He has already had to cope with his parents admitting to extra-marital affairs, the publication of the 'Squidgy' tapes involving his mother and the 'Camillagate' tapes which feature his father fantasizing about being a tampon.

Prince William's future is very much tied up in the debate over primogeniture. And that debate, in turn, is much coloured by the question as to whether his father, the Prince of Wales, should continue to be heir to the throne.

In his favour it can be said that he is perceived to have an awareness of spiritual matters. Jonathan Dimbleby gives this account of Charles's early spiritual development:

Living under the shadow of his mother's consecration at her coronation as 'the defender of Christ's religion', the Prince's faith had at first seemed to be as conventional as the apostles of the Established Church would expect from the heir apparent. At Gordonstoun he had sought comfort in what he had then described as the 'mystery' of the Church.

In preparation for Confirmation he was diligent and receptive, far more so than many would-be communicants of his age. According to the school chaplain, the Revd Philip Crosfield, he showed no inclination to challenge the certainties of the Apostolic Creed. Crosfield detected that as a young teenager the Prince was 'very lost and very lonely'. He also noticed how readily he responded in class to lessons about nature and 'the universal world'...

Charles found his brief period of schooling in Australia in 1965 a liberation and a confidence booster. He became keen to discover values and strengths in cultures – and faiths – other than those into which he had been born. During the late seventies, Charles's spiritual journey led him to study works of mysticism from several different faiths. Unhappy as he was with scientific explanations of existence, Charles was deeply impressed and inspired by the coherence of the answers which mystics from the Hindu and Buddhist traditions and elsewhere had found to the central questions of human existence. However, despite the benefits to him personally, was it a suitable course for a prospective Supreme Governor of the Church of England to take? Jonathan Dimbleby gives this account of Charles's dilemma:

His pursuit of self-discovery through the alternative dogmas of other religions put his own commitment to the Church of England severely to the test. Though he would never sever the bonds, he stretched them to the limit, concluding only latterly that 'one should not move too far from one's culture'. This venture was a stepping stone along a route which led him eventually to declare in public, and with full knowledge of the implications, that, as sovereign, he would hope to be 'Defender of Faith' rather than 'Defender of *the* Faith'.

This would not presumably preclude Prince Charles from taking his full part as Sovereign within the established churches of England

and Scotland. As a confirmed member of the Church of England, he would be able to continue to take part in acts of worship and take Communion. The Church of England would no doubt tolerate his other religious idiosyncrasies in much the same way as it tolerates its own priests who are also Quakers or members of other organizations with spiritual interests. He might, however, find himself in conflict with certain evangelicals who, in particular, deplore the Church's involvement in multi-faith occasions. There would undoubtedly be petitions should King Charles III encourage too great an involvement by Muslims and Hindus in Commonwealth ceremonials, and should the future King take full part in an act of worship arranged by another faith, he would predictably receive irate correspondence. But, then again, he received some poisonous letters from certain Protestants when he went to Rome and was entertained by the Pope.

Charles has the broadest of understandings of the word 'faith' which he has brought to bear in his public concerns for the environment, the planet and architecture. He wrote in this vein about the architectural establishment, with whom he has clashed on many occasions.

I want the Institute to teach its students *reverence* – reverence for the landscape and the soil; for the human spirit which is a reflection in some small measure of the Divine; and for the *grammar* of architecture which, as in a language, enables an infinite variety of forms to be expressed within the context of harmonized sentences...

'In that short note,' comments Jonathan Dimbleby, 'Prince Charles spontaneously wove together the complementary themes which had been with him, growing in clarity and definition, for most of his adult life: man's identity within the natural world; the correspondence of the natural world with the idea of God; the expression of God within the human spirit; and the potential for architecture to give physical form to those sublime relationships.'

Although apparently aware of the danger of straying too far from his own religious and cultural roots, Charles is clearly uncomfortable with the narrowness of the religious role allocated to the British Sovereign. In particular, he regrets that the three great monotheistic religions of the world – Judaism, Christianity and Islam – have so often behaved as enemies.

He has also shown dismay at the schisms within the Christian communion. In particular, as he had demonstrated so forcibly in his attempt to attend mass in the Pontiff's private chapel during his official visit to Italy in 1985, he was contemptuous of doctrinal and liturgical disputes that divided the Roman from the Anglican Church. As a scion of the House of Tudor, his attitude towards King Henry VIII's repudiation of the authority of Pope Leo X, who had bestowed on him the title of Defender of the Faith in 1521, was far from reverential. Charles observed at the time that Henry VIII had broken from Rome essentially because the Pope had refused to sanction his divorce, yet kept the title 'Defender of the Faith' which the Pope had earlier conferred on him simply because he liked it.

The emergence of the Anglican Church, as the Prince was well aware, was a more fraught and intricate process than this; yet it was in such terms that he chose to remember the establishment of the Church of England. Taken together, his belief in the contiguity of the monotheistic religions and his impatience with inter-denominational disputations had come to form the bedrock of his conviction that salvation springs less from religion than from faith. Jonathan Dimbleby quotes Charles as saying:

'All the great prophets, all the great thinkers, all those who have achieved an awareness of the aspects of life which lie beneath the surface, all have showed the same understanding of the universe or the nature of God or of the purpose of our existence – and that is why I think it is so important to understand the common threads which link us all in one great and important tapestry.'

Jonathan Dimbleby is, of course, one of the Prince's chosen champions – one of the enemy camp, as the Princess might say. In practice, doubt has to be cast over the genuineness of the prince's spiritual search. Is his spiritual sensitivity really compatible with some of his other activities? He has been a member of the armed services and still much enjoys the macho company of the military officer class. He hunts and shoots and has taught his sons these skills. He likes aeroplanes and helicopters and modern cars. All these he has as perks of his position, and he appears to take full advantage of them without a twinge of conscience. This put-down was quoted in Valerie Grove's *Times* interview with the Queen's biographer:

> Prince Charles, in Ms Bradford's view, is 'obviously a sweet, good-natured person, not as clever as he thinks he is, who has been spoiled by his entourage and undermined by his parents'.

Prince Charles busies himself today with a wide range of seemingly contradictory activities, but ought we inflict, as the *Guardian* asked back in 1969, on any man or woman of whatever calibre, a lifetime dedicated to what in essence is a non-job? Or is his predicament best summed up in the words of Sarah Bradford that Charles is a 'victim of his royal birthright. He seems unwilling to accept...that there is a price to pay for privilege – and the greater the privilege, the higher the price.'

But can he be blamed? Surely to be a royal, despite the seeming wealth can only bring unhappiness? This century alone many European monarchs, some the Prince's own kith and kin, have been murdered, ruthlessly deposed, mocked and shunned. Many of those surviving live remote, unreal lives. As Sarah Bradford said of Prince Charles's mother, 'the fact that she is the Queen sets her apart from everyone, even her own children'.

It may well be that, should Parliament review the succession, it is decided that Prince Charles is the most suitable heir, whatever his faults. There have been plenty of monarchs before him far worse. But he should be chosen, it can be strongly argued, on the condition that no assumption be made about Prince William succeeding in turn until Parliament and the people have had the opportunity to examine the matter.

While Parliament is about such business, another very simple curiosity involving the succession could be addressed. That introduced in an earlier and distant age of religious conflict by the 1701 Act of Settlement:

> That all and every Person and Persons that then were, or afterwards should be reconciled to, or should hold Communion with the See or Church of Rome, or should profess the Popish Religion, or marry a Papist, should be excluded, and are by that Act made for ever incapable to inherit, possess or enjoy the Crown and Government of this Realm and Ireland, and the Dominions thereunto belonging, or any part of the same, or to have, use, or exercise any Regal Power, Authority or Jurisdiction within the same; And in all and every such Case and Cases the People of these Realms shall be and are thereby absolved of their Allegiance: And that the said Crown and Government shall from time to time descend to and be enjoyed by such Person or Persons, being Protestants, as should have inherited and enjoyed the same, in any case the said Person or Persons, so reconciled holding Communion, professing, or marrying as aforesaid were naturally dead...

Even the traditional monarchist, the constitutionalist Lord St John of Fawsley accepts that a simple Act of Parliament could bring about an intended change to this. It would at a stroke remove from the statute books what many Roman Catholics – and Lord St John himself perhaps – feel to be an insult to the Queen's British subjects who are also Roman Catholics and see no conflict in this.

Regrettably, such a move would not please everyone, and the Protestants of Northern Ireland might feel aggrieved. How they might be accommodated within constitutional reform will be examined later.

That change to the 1701 Act aside, it is hard to see where the opposition to the ending of primogeniture might come from, especially if it is seen as an opportunity to revive the fortunes of the House of Windsor. Many will argue, however, that it would merely be a fruitless exercise in rearranging the deck chairs on the Windsor Titanic, already doomed to sink.

# 6

# *The Queen of Hearts*

'All couples on their wedding day are royal couples.' No one on that summer's day in 1981 disagreed with the Archbishop of Canterbury. Millions around the world watched on television as the Prince of Wales married his young, virgin bride. The day could have been invented and scripted by the bride's step-grand-mother, the romantic novelist Dame Barbara Cartland.

'Those who are married,' Archbishop Runcie continued, 'live happily ever after the wedding day if they persevere in the real adventure which is the royal task of creating each other and creating a more loving world.'

The Archbishop's address, both religious and serious, as well as being sentimentally appropriate to the general mood of the day, would have suited Walter Bagehot who said that, 'A princely marriage is the brilliant edition of universal fact, and, as such, it rivets mankind... A royal family sweetens politics by the season-able addition of nice and pretty events.'

What Bagehot could never have anticipated is that, in these days of mass communication, a 'pretty event' means a 'televisual event'. As was to be expected from the British monarchy after so many years of careful practice, the wedding was superbly staged and the cameras were given every encouragement to seek out the most moving and spectacular pictures. 'The climax in St Paul's Cathedral,' as described by John Pearson in *The Ultimate Family*, 'was not so much the "purest Strauss" of Princess Anne's wedding five years earlier, as a royal grand opera, complete with state trumpeters, accompanying orchestra and the operatic *prima donna*, Kiri te Kanawa – and it was acted out with a splendour and panache no other family on earth could equal.'

St Paul's Cathedral resounded with joyful music. The nation hung out flags and invested in souvenir mugs and programmes. The tabloid newspapers gushed with enthusiasm about the wedding dress. Yet it is now generally acknowledged that the fairy-tale wedding between the 'handsome' prince and his shy young virgin bride, celebrated with national rejoicing and blessed by the Church, was a sham.

This realization took shape only slowly. Over the years, however, the stories trickled out. There were unsubstantiated and (at the time) unpublished rumours that Prince Charles had spent the eve of his wedding with Camilla Parker-Bowles at Buckingham Palace. Eventually, after the publication of Andrew Morton's biography of the Princess and the announcement of a separation, the true facts emerged. Whatever hopes the Prince might have had at the outset, the marriage quickly failed. It was only a few days into the honeymoon, according to one school of thought, that Diana began to realize that her prince was not a character from a fairy-tale, but an heir to a throne who was obliged by his family to find a partner but who was not truly in love.

Many people have unhappy marriages, and undoubtedly there would have been much sympathy for the couple, but for one additional factor. Even when it was generally acknowledged by the whole family and Palace structure that the marriage was all but dead, the British public was still being fed the fairy-tale. It was this, arguably, which finally caused the public disillusionment. It has become apparent that the Palace has lied frequently and habitually in the past in order to maintain the façade of the model family.

It is this dishonesty which arguably has caused the royal family to fall so far in the public's esteem. Earlier this century, the

House of Windsor invented a new role for itself to justify its special standing and privilege. This role was to represent for the nation the perfect family and embody the ideals of Christian marriage. Thus it was that an errant King declaring his love for a twice divorced American had to be forced into exile. Later, that King's niece, the Queen's sister, in her own words 'mindful of the Church's teaching', had to agree to part from the man she loved.

It appears that the current generation's deviations from the Christian ideal are not as they were in the past, regrettable aberrations which were quickly put right, but normal behaviour for the House of Windsor. Thus, any claims that the House can make to represent Christian virtues are undermined. It is now the case that three of the Queen's four children have experienced broken marriages. The fourth, in the old language of the Church and in a term familiar to the older generation of subjects is 'living in sin'. A forgiving British public would even be prepared to sympathize with this if it were not for the way in which, added to the marriage failures, there has been a large dose of hypocrisy. For it is now seen by many that the Prince and Princess of Wales were not in love when they married – or at least that love was very much one-sided – that Prince Charles had a mistress, and that the romance of the royal wedding was little more than shallow hype.

To put it harshly, in order for the House of Windsor to maintain its dynasty and reproduce itself, the heir to the throne, who had sown his wild oats but carefully steered clear of marriage, needed to find an innocent brood mare to conceive and carry a next generation. Lady Diana Spencer fitted the bill. She was a pretty young virgin, who was assumed to know about palace life, who came from within the magic circle of friends and courtiers, and who was expected to be both fertile and uncomplaining. At least, looking back, this is now a commonly held perception of how the Windsors assessed the bride. Certainly it is thought a great deal of pressure was put on Charles by the family to find a wife to enable him to perpetuate the dynasty.

However, if that was the plan, it has now gone very wrong. Not least because of the way in which an image of Diana has developed which none of the Windsors foresaw. The marriage hype worked all too well, in that Diana became the most popular member of the royal family. She was young, shy, charming, attractive, and in almost every way different from the family into which she had married. Despite the allegations that have been made against her that she is temperamental, psychiatrically unbalanced and disloyal to the monarchy, something about her image still holds sway. She has retained the affections of the British people and the world at large. More than that, she has succeeded in redefining one of the royal family's traditional roles – that of good works.

What the Windsors misjudged was the potential for a new member to bring her new magic to their tarnished and increasingly drab version of monarchy and eclipse it. In some ways, Diana has consciously or unconsciously regenerated the mystique of the monarchy through her work and appearance. She embodies many of the potent images of traditional religion. While formal Christian institutions are on the decline, notions of spirituality are not. There is a turning back to old, often pre-Christian ideas and eternal religious myth. Perhaps it is something inherent in the human psyche that societies need to believe their rulers are in touch with the gods. If this is no longer believed of the House of Windsor at large, much of this element of monarchy, it could be said, has been re-applied to Diana.

As Camille Paglia identified in an article in the *Guardian* in 1992, Diana embodies five potent myths, two of which are deeply and anciently spiritual.

The first of the five myths is that Diana was the Cinderella, the humble nursery school nurse who married the world's most eligible bachelor. Next, Camille Paglia says, she epitomizes the betrayed wife, wronged by a callous husband and his long-standing lover. Thirdly, Diana is characterized by what Camille Paglia describes as a 'boyish androgyny'; she presents an ethereal image which can be traced back to classical times.

However, the two 'spiritual' myths are arguably the most potent: she is on the one hand 'the Mater Dolorosa', the suffering mother, and on the other, she is the pagan goddess, and in this context most suitably named.

Camille Paglia's article, in part a review of Andrew Morton's bestselling book on the Princess of Wales, attributes Diana's image as the suffering mother to the widely noted physical tenderness she has been seen to show towards her children.

'It is ironic,' Paglia wrote, 'that Charles, who plucked Diana from obscurity and who has all the weight of rank and wealth behind him, seems helpless in the court of popular opinion against the ancient archetype of the sorrowing mother or Mater Dolorosa, which Christianity borrowed from the cult of Isis. Charles had sought and found, in Morton's words, 'a virginal Protestant aristocrat to be his bride' only to discover that his philandering attempts to remain himself produced a new Catholic Madonna, a modern Mary with a taste for rock'n'roll.'

Many Roman Catholic faithful are amazed, inspired and delighted when statues of the mother of Jesus appear to weep. One American tabloid is reported to have added a tear streak to photographs of Diana to enhance the image of sorrow so that her marketable pictures came to resemble a 'Spanish Baroque Madonna with precious crystal tears sparkling down her cheeks'. Like a weeping Madonna, Diana has become an object of adoration and fascination with the potential both to excite and divide a crowd.

Claims of miracles, including prophecy, have also been attributed to Diana. It is said she has premonitions of death and predicted her own father's stroke.

Identifying the pagan goddess ingredient in Diana's image, Camille Paglia draws on the world of classical drama and legend. Her conflict with Camilla Parker-Bowles is seen as Diana, the fierce Italian goddess of the woods, versus Camilla, the Amazon, the militant horsewoman.

A photo in Morton's book shows the young Diana Spencer dreamily reading a hunting magazine, *The Field: The Stalking Review*, with grazing stags on its cover. The caption informs us, 'While she has a reputation for being unenthusiastic about blood sports, Diana does enjoy stag hunting.' Throughout art history, the ancient Diana, hot on the chase with her dogs, is almost invariably depicted with a stag or doe. Do names contain their own fate?

Colourful and fanciful prose, perhaps, but revealing if one accepts the universality of legend across time and space. And no more powerful deed can trigger a legend than young death or martyrdom. Prince Charles, it is said, has often accused her of feigning 'martyrdom'. Her dramatic suicide attempts have been reported and one can only speculate on the powerful potential of a Diana cult if the Princess should by any ill chance meet an early end. She would no doubt become a figure as powerful as Evita, President Kennedy and Elvis Presley combined.

Perhaps part of her present hold on the public imagination lies in an impression she gives that she is already a living martyr, a woman imprisoned by the uncaring demands of a royal household. Camille Paglia argues that the restrictions of Diana's existence have helped to create her unique appeal.

The House of Windsor still functions like a studio in the way it sequesters its stars and subjects them to inhumane rules that make them more than human. Although she is still called 'Di' in America, as if she were magically ever-virgin, Diana at her marriage ceased to be a private person and became Her Royal Highness, the Princess of Wales, one in a long succession of women holding that title. She merged with her function. Similarly, the movements of the royals are recorded daily in *The Times* under the rubric of their residences, as if the palace itself has a greater living authority.

Diana's enormous glamour springs from the tension between energy and structure. Going about her public duties, she radiates a magnetic power that is directly produced by her disciplined containment within class and rank. Her staggering worldwide popularity demonstrates the enduring power and significance of hierarchy, a power that fashionable academic paradigms – influenced by feminism, Marxism, Foucault, and the Frankfurt School – cannot understand and whose enduring mystique can only be explained by Roman Catholicism or Hollywood history.

Diana's sole contemporary parallel as an international pop diva is the second Madonna, who, like Diana, expresses herself best through dance, the universal language. Both Diana and Madonna have trouble with words, which fail them in public. Diana even stumbled over her wedding vows, when she reversed the order of Charles' names. It is remarkable how Diana has projected her personality without the use of words. Photographs and video footage are her medium. She may be the last of the silent film stars...

Diana's classical dance training has given her an aplomb and distinction of carriage that make for great photographs even when she is simply getting in and out of cars – a talent conspicuously lacking in the lumbering, bottom-heavy Sarah Ferguson. Like the great stars of the Hollywood studio era, Diana exists for us as primarily a visual presence.

And she is all the more powerful for that. It is possible for words to be picked over and turned back on the speaker or writer to undermine that which they are trying to say. The visual image is immune from such criticism, and the viewer can make of it whatever they will. Despite her masterful employment of language in her 'Panorama' interview, there were phrases which her critics seized upon to weaken her cause. It was her expression and her doleful eyes which made a lasting impression on the viewers.

So it is that the visual presence of Diana not only sells maga-
zines but is very much in demand by charities wishing to borrow
some of the 'magic'. Yet it is an image which is mutually contradictory. How can Cinderella become the sorrowing mother,
how can the pagan goddess be, at the same time, the martyred
saint?

> Deification has its costs. The modern mega-celebrity, bear-
> ing the burden of collective symbolism, projection, and fan-
> tasy, is a ritual victim, cannibalized by our pity and fear.
> Those at the apex of the social pyramid are untouchables,
> condemned to horrifying solitude. There may have been
> many unhappy wives in royal history, but they did not have
> to live their emotions under the minute scrutiny of the tele-
> photo lens. Mass media have made both myth and disaster
> out of Diana's story.

Yet from the media wreckage Diana has risen, her supporters
would say, like a phoenix from the ashes. She has come to learn
how to manipulate the media and trust none of the official royal
advisers. She has created photo-opportunities which have helped
substantiate her cause and planted cleverly devised scoops in the
newspapers to confound those in the royal circle she sees as out to
get her and demean her. Her television interview on 'Panorama'
was as deft a public relations coup as any professional could have
devised. And then, more lethal and devastating to the 'enemy'
than anything else, has been her behind-the-scenes tending of the
sick.

Most of her visits are private affairs, but enough of the veil is
lifted on her work for people to know what she is about. Like
Evita and other powerful semi-mythological women before her
who have been adored by the public, she is also able to live a
double life. She does good work in disguise late at night with
AIDS patients on the one hand, and yet can jet off to holidays in
the sun, look beautiful and have glamorous clothes on the other.

She is able to present herself as fallible, mortal, weak and vulnerable and can be readily forgiven, as long as she turns that vulnerability to good effect by offering what she has to those in greater need. When Prince Charles admitted to his affair with Camilla Parker-Bowles it was a scandal. When Diana acknowledged her extra-marital relationship, she was able to get away with her admission with little harm being done to her image. She allowed people to sympathize with her for having been twice misled and then let down by a heartless man.

Looking back at the history of religion, especially when bound up with powerful political and social forces, it is not beyond the bounds of possibility that a powerful myth may develop around stories of Diana the healer. Claims will be made that her touch has brought not only relief but remission to the sick. Already in the popular press this is taking shape. In January 1996, in the American tabloid weekly *National Examiner*, an article by Diana Johnson appeared which could well set the pattern for the future.

Princess Diana believes she has the healing power of angels in her fingertips – and she's using her God-given gift to help the gravely ill during hush-hush hospital visits.

'Di is convinced her touch can cure the sick,' says the pretty royal's personal psychic, Betty Palko. 'She's blessed.'

Insiders say the princess's Florence Nightingale missions have given her life new spiritual meaning – following months of tears and trouble.

'I feel the power of God working through my fingertips,' Di confided to a close friend. 'I feel like I have been chosen for this work. I hear a thundering voice from on high telling me to continue to do these good deeds.

'This sort of work brings me strength. I'm drawn to it. And the strength of the patients is incredible.'

Diana's still reeling from the queen's command for her to divorce Prince Charles, but she won't let it stop her work with the tragically ill – and her reputation as a healer is growing every day, says the friend.

'At first, it was just a small circle of people who knew the princess possesses some kind of magical ability to help cure the sick,' says her pal. 'But as more patients improved after being touched by Diana, it became obvious to everyone what was happening.'

It's a closely guarded secret, but she has already cured hundreds of children who surely would have died without her healing power.

'I wouldn't be surprised if someday the princess awoke to find a long line of sufferers outside her door,' her pal says.

'Years from now, when people are traveling from all over the world to be healed by her hands, she may even be considered a saint.'

Ironically, the princess believes that in a previous life she was a nun who was treated cruelly by superstitious people who mistook her for a witch, says psychic Betty.

But in this lifetime, the Lord is rewarding her for kindness toward others by giving her the power to heal.

'She will definitely be a person like Mother Teresa. She is so gentle in her heart and is such a wonderful healer,' says the psychic, who has helped Di through her darkest hours. 'Diana just cares so much about others.'

But the princess is desperately trying to keep her missions of mercy under wraps so she can work her miracles without hordes of admirers and cameras following her every move. She's been seen leaving hospitals long after dark in jeans, a sweatshirt and baseball cap, begging the staff to guard the patients' privacy.

'These people, cancer patients or people with other illnesses, come out of the operating room and awake alone. All I want to do is be there with them,' the modest royal admits. 'I hold their hands, I chat with them – whatever they need I give them. And they all need to be loved.'

The American tabloids enjoy stretching a good story to its limits and the tales of Saint Di published on the other side of the Atlantic have to be taken with a pinch of salt. The value in quoting it however is to demonstrate how the mythology of Diana is beginning to grow. What will matter in years to come is not what is true, but what people believe to be true. In Britain there have been similar, if perhaps less sensational 'bedside exposés' showing Diana to have the healing, or at least soothing, touch. This comes from the *Daily Mail* in January 1996 and concerns a tiny baby boy Diana had held in her arms:

James's parents had spent the first days of his life praying he would live. Suffering serious heart and lung problems, he was taken to London from a hospital in Southend within hours of his birth.

His mother Anne Pearce and her parents Brian and Rosemary were sitting by his cot in the Royal Brompton hospital when Diana arrived unannounced on the children's ward. 'She just walked over and started chatting,' said his mother. 'She asked what his name was and what was wrong with him. Then she said, "Can I pick him up?"

'I said "Yes," and she ignored all the heart monitors, the oxygen feed and other tubes and gently lifted him out.

'She asked me how much he weighed at birth and when I told her 6lbs 1oz she said one of her boys was the same. Then she said "Just big enough really, before it starts to hurt."

'She said James was gorgeous and had lovely hair. She spent several minutes chatting with us and holding him. She was so gentle with him that he slept right through his royal audience.

'He was the youngest on the ward and the only one she picked up. Her visit was the talk of the ward for the rest of the day. There were queues of patients waiting to use the phone to tell their families.

'She may not be able to heal people but she can give them comfort and take people's minds off their problems, if only for a short time. The whole thing was totally natural and unplanned. She lifted everyone's spirits.

'It was great for my parents as much as anything because it had been a dreadful six days for them. They had been terribly upset and the Princess's appearance made everything so much better...

'She can't heal people but she brings them great comfort...She drives up unannounced in her car alone and walks on to the ward. She seems to understand the nature of all the illnesses.

'There is one boy on the ward who is quite sick but she apparently always sits on the end of his bed and eats all his Maltesers. Apparently it makes his day.'

Her visit to James came just hours before Diana broke down and wept after being pursued by freelance photographers leaving the home of her therapist Susie Orbach.

Some observers have questioned her charitable intentions since she expressed her wish in November's 'Panorama' TV interview to become the 'queen of people's hearts'.

But James's grandfather defended her staunchly. 'This was not pre-arranged,' he said. 'She wasn't trying to make anything out of the visit. She didn't know I was going to ask to take her photograph. She simply wanted to give people a lift.

'She was relaxed and a natural mother judging by the way she handled James. There has been a lot of talk about what her role should be in life. After watching her, I feel there must be something she can do with children, be it fundraising or being a figurehead. She has such natural ability.'

What appears to have happened is that Diana has taken a traditional royal function, extended it and all but monopolized it. Only once has her image as the carer been slightly tarnished, when she watched open heart surgery being performed on a child – giving Sky television exclusive access to televize the event. The 'enemy' grabbed the opportunity to brief the press that she had gone too far in lending her name and reputation to such a tacky stunt.

For many years, the royal family has patronized charities and encouraged voluntary work, especially where the sick are involved. This was well documented by Frank Prochaska in his recent work *Royal Bounty: The Making of a Welfare Monarchy*.

Prochaska wrote of how the constitutional and ceremonial roles of the monarchy have tended to obscure "what was taking place just below the political surface or behind the Palace window dressing. Since the Second World War, the royal family has adapted the tradition, which dates back to George III, of making the monarchy the head and focus of civil society through its welfare work. Beyond that, royal philanthropy serves well the monarchy's wider intention of providing the unifying symbol of the nation. Yet the significance of the social side of the monarchy's national role through its promotion of welfare causes is largely lost on the Crown's defenders, who, having read little since Bagehot, continue to dwell on those familiar nostrums of magic and high politics.

When republicans assemble they too dwell on high politics and the constitution, while lingering over the costs, the scandals and the symbolism of royalty. Whatever the merits of their case, they, like the monarchists, leave the monarchy's welfare role out of the equation. Certainly, the abolition of the crown would create a presidential system, turn 'subjects' into 'citizens', and save public money, though perhaps only in the short term. Beyond that lies greater uncertainty. In this debate, as in so much else in politics, temperament is fate. But if there is a lesson from the past, it is that reform usually has unforeseen and unintended consequences. For the circumspect, who share the crown's suspicion of what Prince Albert described as 'exceedingly

expensive' political experiments, the dangers of republicanism seem real enough, the benefits less obvious. If Britain
did become a republic, it would be an unhappy irony if its
'citizens' found themselves with fewer civil liberties than
they had enjoyed as 'subjects' of the crown.

Britain's philanthropic traditions, so instrumental in civic
life and liberty, are profound. The crown's contribution to
these traditions has been and continues to be enabling. The
abolition of the monarchy, whatever the benefits, would
mark another stage in the perfection of the state monolith.
Moreover, it would eliminate that part of the constitution
that serves as a buffer between the state and society. It could
be argued that this is a role that an elected president could
not sustain nor endure. To be sure, the United States has a
vibrant voluntary sector without a monarchy, but it has
developed its own charitable customs within a quite different social, fiscal and constitutional context. The first lady,
however many her charities, cannot be compared to the
Queen as a focus of civil society.

Republicans and monarchists alike would do well to recall
the line of Dr Johnson:

> How small, of all that human hearts endure,
> That part which laws of kings can cause or cure!

Undoubtedly, Britain's voluntary traditions would survive a
republic, as they have survived religious decline and the
ascendant state. Still, the abolition of the monarchy would
destabilize thousands of existing institutions, many of them
with royal charters. Where would they turn to steady their
finances and to reassure their supporters and those who
depend on their services – to the president? If to the state,
it would only further increase its costs, and its influence, at
the expense of their independence. But this is academic, for
barring cataclysm or self-destruction, the monarchy is only

likely to be in real danger when the begging letters cease to arrive at Buckingham Palace.

What Prochaska did not address is what might happen when the letters that arrive at Buckingham Palace are increasingly addressed to the Princess of Wales, the royal outsider. No official statistics are ever released, but it would be fair to speculate that already she receives far more requests for visits and patronage than her husband. It was suggested that one of the factors in the breakdown of the Wales's marriage was that Charles could not cope with the crowds wanting to see his wife and not him. Even the Prince's champion Jonathan Dimbleby concedes this. He describes a visit the couple made to Australia in the early days of their marriage, noting Charles's resentment that the crowds were screaming for 'Lady Di'. By the time of the last visit by Diana to Balmoral for Christmas, things had swung so far it is said that after morning church the Queen was ushered out of a back door so as not to be embarrassed by the press corps who did not want to take pictures of her, but of the Princess of Wales.

What might the consequences of all this be? Whatever happens to the House of Windsor, Diana, her supporters suggest, will survive. Indeed, as was suggested earlier, if by some unfortunate event she should die young, the myth would become so strong that it would undoubtedly eclipse that of Elvis Presley and other twentieth-century media stars who died prematurely. That is not designed to be a flippant comparison, for Diana is no longer merely an actor in a royal soap opera or the latest ornament of the House of Windsor or solely the property or interest of the British people, but an international media phenomenon.

One of the solutions which has been talked about to lance the Windsor boil is that Prince William become King ahead of his father. This may indeed give the Windsors that break with the past and its unhappy present it so badly needs. If this were the case, the figure of Princess Diana would be all powerful. She might be styled Queen Diana, her son as King would have the authority to do so. She certainly, according to the press reports, fought long and hard with her husband's lawyers over the divorce settlement to make sure it enables her to keep her royal style.

Diana feels she needs this style for her sons because, when William becomes King, she would have a claim to direct access to him. This she does not want to lose. No wonder Diana's major obsession today is that her sons are not wooed away from her and that they are not encouraged to prefer the company of their father and the effervescent Tiggy to her own. But it seems from the evidence that has been released that there is a touching affection and concern shown by the sons – Prince William in particular – for their mother. William appears to be a solemn young man aware of a great responsibility on his shoulders. It would surely be an act of cruelty to put him on the throne at too young an age. In all probability, if he were to become King at a young age, he would reign for a very long time, and there is no evidence in British history that there is anything to be gained from a long-serving monarch.

A daring extension of this idea is one which would be more vigorously opposed by the Windsors than any other, but might find favour with the British people. Suppose William became King on the understanding that he does not assume full responsibilities until, say, the age of thirty. In that case, a regent would need to be appointed. Who better than the new King's mother, Queen Regent Diana?

The Prince William solution is perhaps an unlikely one. He may well succeed ahead of his father, but only through natural causes if his grandmother should live to a ripe old age and she should outlive his father. What is more likely is that a divorced Diana, re-married or not, will continue to build up her image as the healer and carer. In this role she will be a constant rival to the House of Windsor and reminder that it has lost its magic touch. If, as is proposed below, one of the other solutions to the Windsor problem be adopted,

Diana will still always be there and she will evolve into a graceful old lady much admired and even deified by the population. The 'enemy' will try and undermine this image, but provided she does nothing outrageous – and a marriage to someone deemed unsuitable would be included here – she is unlikely to lose her mystique.

This mystique will survive especially if Diana does remain unmarried and retains her title. She might throw herself into creating a hospital or a charity. She might take on some religious vows, albeit of a non-traditional kind. She might gather round her a group of advisers and gurus who will feed her with all sorts of notions about who she is and what her destiny might be. Given the approaching millennium and the growing interest in spiritual ideas in the nation, who knows where that might lead. There might almost be a Diana cult.

It is far-fetched speculation, perhaps, although what can be said with certainty is that one of the only two members of the royal family who can still claim any form of magic is among the newest. The other is the oldest, Queen Elizabeth the Queen Mother. While both women married in and provided the House of Windsor with a much-needed boost from the outside, today only one can claim still to be one of the inner circle. Diana is on the outside.

Nevertheless the Diana image is a potent force. Because it has that element of magic and mystery which the Windsors have lost, it is one the 'enemy' has no way of resisting. Even an admission of adultery and the publication of the 'Squidgy' tapes has done little to dent the myth. Not since the days when it was believed that by merely touching the Monarch one could be healed of certain diseases, has the 'royal touch' been seen in action.

When the Queen visits hospitals in the conventional manner it is an event planned months or years in advance. All the Trust members, administrators and consultants line up to shake her hand and exchange a few bland pleasantries. A ribbon is cut or a plaque unveiled. The Queen walks along specially cleaned and decorated corridors, the county's Lord Lieutenant at her side. The duty photographers on the royal rota take dull pictures. The

Queen seldom smiles and never cradles babies. It is the same with most of the other Windsors. On the other hand Diana arrives after hours, almost unannounced, except via one or two anonymous telephone tip-offs to the tabloids, wearing a baseball cap and casual clothes. She holds people's hands and, what is far more, she is frequently seen to be embracing those whose illnesses carry social stigma.

While the Princess Royal has taken a down-to-earth view through her work with the Save the Children fund, it is in the interests of the Princess of Wales not to discourage the mystery which surrounds her life and work. She knows instinctively how to make a news story, whether by releasing little bits of unofficial information, or turning a public function into a special moment. Every time television clips of her holding the hands of AIDS patients or allowing a blind man to feel her face and pronounce her to be the most beautiful person in the world are shown, they contribute towards an image of the Princess as some form of mystical healer. No claims need to be made. She plays on the needs of ordinary people for hope and romance. There is no firm evidence that she is unscrupulously scheming. Her tender self is part of her natural self – part of her inner need to be loved, tabloid psychiatrists might say, but it is also an irresistible weapon in her armoury. She is talked of as having some of the Mother Teresa qualities, and myth and legend are growing up around her. If the fall of the Windsors from grace has left a vacuum in the affections of the British people and left them starved and cheated of the magic of the monarchy, Diana could well be filling that void. Whether she recognizes it as such or not, hers has become a quasi-religious calling.

Yet the Princess of Wales has not been seen to embrace conventional Christianity, at least not of the Anglican variety. The tabloid press talks of her interests in alternative medicine and her supposed need to consult clairvoyants. She believes in reincarnation, as was revealed in the 'Squidgy' tapes. If there is mention in public circles of her faith, it is often in the form of speculation about how she might join the Church of Rome in a direct violation of the British Monarch's Protestant obligations. It was suggested at one point that Diana had sought instruction from a fashionable Roman Catholic priest, but unless she springs a surprise on her public and announces a conversion, it is probably best to assume that dabbling with Rome was just one of her many passing fads.

Through her, the monarchy retains some of its religious inheritance. She is bringing to the surface the ancient archetypes of monarchy which had been covered over by Anglican respectability and the State religion which had dominated the coronation of the Queen over forty years earlier. Diana's persona is powerful and religious. She appeals to folk-faith and primitive spirituality. She is simultaneously the Mater Dolorosa, the suffering mother, and the pagan goddess – the unsettling feminine figure in a male-dominated cultural landscape. Hers is a potent, semi-mystical role, and she cannot be totally discarded by the royal family as she is their elect, chosen by them to be mother of the future King.

# 7

# *The Windsors Replaced*

Just over 90 years ago, after five centuries in which it had been attached either to Sweden or to Denmark, Norway became an independent nation. In drawing up the new constitution there was considerable discussion as to whether the newly independent nation should be a republic or a monarchy. After much debate it was settled that a new Norwegian Crown be established and the second son of the Danish Crown Prince was asked to become King. Prince Carl of Denmark became the new Norwegian King Haakon VII when his accession to the throne was confirmed by a substantial majority at a referendum.

He reigned for 52 years. He died in 1957, was succeeded by Olav V, who in turn was succeeded in 1991 by King Harald V.

Haakon VII was elected King of Norway on 18 November 1905 and crowned at Trondheim Cathedral on 22 June the next year. The coronation was, in fact, more of an installation, and was described as a very dignified if simple affair which set the tone for the long reign of the first King of the new, independent Norway.

Not that the King's other royal relations were much impressed by this low-key accession to what was seen as a dangerously democratic and revolutionary throne. The coronation was attended by Britain's future King George V and Queen Mary since the new Queen of Norway was to be Princess Maud, one of Queen Victoria's daughters. When one of her relations suggested to

Queen Mary that a revolutionary coronation was a farce, she replied, 'The whole thing seems curious, but we live in very modern days.'

The lesson to be drawn from the Norwegian experience is that it is quite possible, given the will of the people, for a nation to invite a suitable family to take over the role of constitutional monarch. If it should be the will of the people of Britain that the House of Windsor be invited to retire and a new, low-key form of constitutional monarchy be introduced in their stead, the Norwegian precedent might be a good one to follow. It was found to be the consensus of the time that a monarchy was desirable and preferable to a presidency; a suitable candidate was found and approached; he indicated his willingness to perform the part; and, at a vote of the people, his position was endorsed.

To those who might suppose that such a handover of a throne can only happen in Scandinavia, the events of 1714 should provide a reminder that the principle of a family from overseas being invited to cross the water in order to take over the throne has a precedent here in Britain. *Burke's Royal Families of the World* describes the circumstances of the Hanoverian succession like this. The year was 1714. Queen Anne died and George I, a member of a minor German royal family, became King.

It is a pity that the Electress Sophia, who died only two months before Queen Anne, did not live long enough to become Queen of England. That splendid old Princess, who was so proud of her English connexions – with reason, for she was the sister of Prince Rupert the Cavalier, the daughter of 'the Winter Queen' and the niece of Charles I – would have been a far better introduction to the House of Hanover than her boorish and brutish son, George I. When he came to England as King in 1714, the first of the Georges was fifty-four; he was heavy and ungainly, he spoke not a word of English. He had parted from his wife, the unhappy Sophia Dorothea, twenty years earlier, in a sensational scandal involving the murder of her love, Konigsmarck; since then she had been kept shut up in the moated grange of Ahlden. Instead of a Queen, George brought with him two ugly German mistresses, whom the English promptly christened 'the Maypole' and 'the Elephant'. He also brought a posse of German advisers, though these never had any political significance.

However, the popular view of George I is certainly a prejudiced one; for while the majority of Englishmen, like the Vicar of Bray, gave their allegiance to 'The Illustrious House of Hanover and Protestant Succession', they really wanted the Protestant Succession without the House of Hanover, however illustrious; they had already had their bellyful of foreign Kings with Dutch William. Hanoverian George was not only a foreigner, but his talents were not such as appealed to the English genius. He was a soldier, pure and simple, and a brave one; but the English still regarded the professional military man with suspicion. For commerce, the arts and science, literature and religious and political discussion, the chief interests of a generation that had founded the Bank of England, produced Wren and Newton, Swift and Defoe, and argued itself stiff over Dr Sacheverell, he had no taste at all. He was, however, musical; Handel composed the *Water Music* in his honour. It was first played when the King went on the Thames from Whitehall to Limehouse, and he was so pleased with it that he gave Handel a pension of £200 a year.

Politically, as is well known, the advent of George led to the Whig Supremacy and to an unintentional curtailment of the Royal Prerogative owing to the King's perpetual absence from meetings of his Cabinet. The Whig Supremacy was partly caused by the fact that the Whigs had put the King under an obligation to them by ensuring his succession; which, despite the provisions of the Act of 1701, was by no means a foregone conclusion; Tory opinion during the reign of Queen Anne having swung back towards the

Pretender. And while the Tory leaders, by their flirtation with 'James III', had given the Whigs a chance of winning George's unfailing gratitude, they had also thereby incurred the stigma of Jacobitism and treason, which effectively kept them out of politics for many years to come.

George's lack of English and his Ministers' of German is generally thought of as the reason why he ceased to preside over his Cabinet, thus leaving the way open for the ascendancy of Sir Robert Walpole, who became the first Prime Minister – though for many years to come, the term was only used opprobriously. But if George had really wanted to attend Cabinet meetings, he and his Ministers could have spoken to each other in French. His frequent absences in Hanover were another reason why he did not attend his Cabinet; and then there was his lack of interest in English politics.

Yet it was not merely George's physical absence from the Cabinet and the country which caused the sharp decline in the Royal Prerogative during his reign. The Monarchy, as Mr Roger Fulford points out, was brought down to earth. To a certain extent, this was due to George's own personality; then, with the setting aside of the legitimate Stuart line, less emphasis could be placed on the divine nature of kingship – it is significant that the Georges ceased to 'touch' for the King's evil. Then, again, it must be remembered that, to their subjects, the first two Georges seemed much less securely established than they do to us, who have hindsight. 'And George my rightful King shall be until the times do alter' was the sentiment of many more Englishmen of those days than just the proverbial Vicar of Bray.

It was not generally held in those days that a dynasty was immovable. Only 29 years earlier, the Stuart line of descent had been broken. It is a contemporary and mistaken assumption to suppose that a royal family cannot be replaced. Certainly, if a change were made today, there need be no fear that the new monarch would be boorish and unable to speak English. There are a number of suitable candidates.

Let it be assumed that agreement has been reached to replace the Windsors, and a date for the abdication of Queen Elizabeth II has been set. How this agreement might be reached will be examined later, but let it be assumed for now that a committee has been appointed by the House of Commons to draw up a list of suitable candidates for the position of Sovereign of the United Kingdom. It might, of course, be at that stage that a decision is taken to allow Scotland to decide the matter separately, and by then a Scottish parliament might be sitting which would appoint a similar committee.

Many centuries earlier, it was possible for a royal house to be drawn from an equally powerful aristocratic house in Britain itself. However, since the days of the Yorks and the Lancasters and of Warwick the Kingmaker, none of the other aristocratic dynasties can compete with the Monarch in wealth or prestige. The Dukes of Buccleuch and Devonshire are great landowners, and the Duke of Westminster is astonishingly wealthy, yet none of them can expect to be accepted by the British people in the place of the House of Windsor. Indeed, if legitimacy is to be claimed from descent, it is necessary to look to Europe for a new candidate since many of the European royal families are descended in one way or another directly from Queen Victoria. The advantage of approaching an established European royal household is that most have already established a way of working and a public image. They have a track record. They might not all be seen cycling around the streets of the capital city, but most have evolved a lifestyle which is far less pretentious, and probably therefore more acceptable, than that associated with the British royal family. They are experienced as constitutional monarchs, and if any one of them chosen to play the part of British constitutional monarch continued in a life style both simple and unostentatious, dividing themselves between duties in the United Kingdom and those in their present country, at a stroke, the British Crown could survive.

So whom might this parliamentary committee of the great and good approach with an offer of the British Crown? There are well over forty royal families, containing both working monarchs and pretenders, living in Europe. They range from the Grand Dukes of such places as Luxembourg to the princely Houses of Monaco of Hohenzollern, from royal houses in exile, like that of Greece, to a number which are still at work. Belgium, Denmark, Sweden, Norway, Holland, Spain, Luxembourg are all countries which have retained the monarchy. All, or almost all, have a close link with Britain and although some have been involved in scandal or political controversy, it would not be too difficult to find a suitable candidate to accede to the British throne.

The job specification would not be too difficult to draw up.

**WANTED** – person to take on the duties of King or Queen of Britain on a part-time basis. Previous royal experience preferable. Must demonstrate suitable dignity in performing basic functions of State (e.g. opening Parliament and handing out honours). Must be free from scandal, have a suitable heir, or family from whom an heir can be chosen, and be prepared to live and work in Britain for a number of weeks a year. It would be an advantage to speak fluent English, be descended from Queen Victoria, have no political ambitions or strong views, and be of a sufficiently mature age not to be likely to reign for too long.

The final requirement would enable the British people to have some time to savour the experiment without the change becoming irreversible. Alternatively, the Crown could be offered for a fixed period of time, renewable by referendum after that period. The requirement to provide a suitable heir could also be modified. It might be that at the end of the reign a new committee would be set up to review a new set of candidates from the royal families of Europe, or decide which of the Monarch's existing children, nephews or nieces would be a suitable successor.

One name that is sure to come to the top of the list is Queen Margarethe II of Denmark. Now 56 years old, with 24 years experience on the throne, she is certainly the most erudite and educated of the current candidates.

On her accession, she became the first female sovereign of Denmark for nearly 600 years. It could indeed be argued that she became Queen by election as well as lineal descent, as some years before her accession a referendum was held in the country and it was decided that she, a woman, would have precedence over the next male heir, Prince Knud.

The Queen speaks Danish, Swedish, English and French fluently, and even has a smattering of Faroese. In her youth, she won a bronze badge at judo and is no mean marksperson with the rifle. Her academic qualifications are equally impressive. She read archaeology and international law at Cambridge, attended the Sorbonne in France, studied sociology at the London School of Economics and studied further at Copenhagen and Aarhus in Denmark.

She was not crowned Queen, as the simpler style of the Danish Monarch requires that she simply be proclaimed by the Prime Minister. She is one of the monarchs who has been rather disparagingly described as a 'cycling monarch'. It has been known for her to go off shopping on her bicycle, but basically she lives a comfortable life carrying out her role as an impartial Head of State with few frills and nothing like the extravagance of the Windsors.

Queen Margarethe's descent from Queen Victoria can also be established. Her father Frederick IX who reigned from 1947 to 1972, married Princess Ingrid, daughter of Gustav VI, King of Sweden. It is therefore through her mother's line that she can trace her lineage to the British throne as her grandfather, King of Sweden, was married to Princess Margaret, the eldest daughter of

Prince Arthur, Duke of Connaught and Strathearn. And Arthur Duke of Connaught, who was born in 1850 and died in 1942, was the seventh of Queen Victoria's children.

Queen Margarethe's husband, Prince Hejnrik of Denmark, was born a French national, and they have two sons now in their twenties. In an interview with Veronica Maclean, Queen Margarethe described how both her sons had spent a period doing military service.

'They entered the army as Privates, were treated exactly like all the other recruits, and had to mix and get on with everyone. They did very well, became sergeants and eventually officers.'

Queen Margarethe works from her eighteenth-century palace in Copenhagen, the Amalienvorg, but lives part of the year at her country palace some 40 miles away. She is a frequent visitor to London, where her sister Anne Marie lives with her husband the exiled King of the Hellenes. Her duties are strictly those of the constitutional monarch which in a modern age she sees as being the guardian of justice and democracy in her country. Her ceremonial duties are few although she is responsible for all decorations, awards and honours given to Danish citizens. She presides over a state council and meets her Prime Minister and Foreign Secretary on a regular basis. She has no formal court but does have a Lord Chamberlain, a Private Secretary and Ladies-in-Waiting when she needs them.

'Her day starts at her desk in Amalienvorg,' Veronica Maclean wrote in her book *Crowned Heads*.

There she reads state documents with her Private Secretary, has consultations, planning meetings and discussions with her Chamberlain. She has a light lunch, sometimes just a sandwich in her upstairs apartment and then there are always engagements in the afternoon. The evenings are usually spent at home, which means with her family.

Her lifestyle is dignified and comparatively affluent but her family can never be said to be guilty of the conspicuous displays of wealth exhibited by the British royal family. She would undoubtedly be a very good model of any future British King or Queen should she not be in the running herself for that position. As the *Observer* once said in a review of European royal talent, 'veteran court correspondents are hard-pressed to find the slightest hint of scandal in the royal house'.

Similarly, the Kings of Sweden and Norway can trace themselves back to Queen Victoria and both families could find themselves providing candidates for the shortlist for the British throne.

Norway's King Harald V is the right age, approaching sixty. Sweden's King Carl XVI Gustaf is ten years younger. Both monarchs have maintained a far simpler court and lifestyle than the Windsors.

In Sweden, even after years of benevolent social democracy which in most countries would have been overseen by a president, the constitutional monarch has survived to retain its ceremonial functions as Head of State. The royal House is that of Bernadotte, which traces its origins back to 1809 and some unusually democratic beginnings. Its history does not go back to a centuries-old aristocratic family but to one of Napoleon's soldiers, Jean-Baptiste Bernadotte, who rose from the ranks to become a marshal. Only three years before his accession he had in fact defeated the Swedes at the Battle of Pomerania, but his humane and enlightened behaviour in victory endeared him to the Swedish people. He was also known independently to have acted as a buffer between Napoleon and the Swedish people, upholding the Swedes' interests. Having been Monarch in all but name for ten years, on the death of the childless Charles VIII in 1818 he formally became King. Interestingly, he spoke very little Swedish, French being his native language, and while acting every inch a king was also proud of his humble origins: he had once been a sergeant in Napoleon's army. Today his 50-year-old descendant Carl XVI Gustaf performs the function of Head of State without any of his illustrious predecessor's extensive powers. There was much talk when he succeeded his grandfather in 1973 that the time was right for the Swedish monarchy to be dissolved, but by the time of his marriage in 1976 and the birth of his children, republicanism had ceased to be a major political issue.

The King of Sweden has probably the least power of any reigning monarch. He acts as a roving ambassador in his country's interests and hands out decorations and orders. Veronica Maclean has argued that he is the country's most wasted asset, an underused king. He is married to Queen Sylvia who is the daughter of a West German businessman. Her mother is Brazilian. Their eldest daughter, Crown Princess Victoria, now 19, is expected to inherit the throne, as in Sweden it is no longer assumed that the eldest son will do so. Victoria is two years older than her brother, Philip. Carl Gustaf is a king who is certainly not as yet thought to have put a foot wrong, and if it is indeed the case that he is underemployed, subsidiary duties as the constitutional Monarch of the new Great Britain could be offered to him.

Across the long Scandinavian border in Norway, King Harald V might also be a suitable candidate for the part-time position. When he assumed the throne, there was no formal crowning, simply a service of blessing in Oslo Cathedral. As for style, he pays taxes, drives a Volvo and has none of the Windsors' assumptions that he should be addressed or dealt with as some sort of special, elevated mortal.

King Harald V served as an army officer and finished his education at Balliol College, Oxford, where he read political science, history and economics. He became Crown Prince on the death of his grandfather in 1957 and immediately began to share the duties of monarchy, attending state council, presiding over committees and even acting as Regent when King Olaf was ill. A very different approach from that of the Windsors, whose eldest sons have been almost entirely excluded from any of the Monarch's functions until they themselves inherit. King Olaf is a frequent visitor to Britain and, of course, like all the Scandinavian monarchs, speaks excellent English. Veronica Maclean's impression of him was that he was a strong, active man, very much in touch with his people. He is also, she wrote, aware of the limitations of his power but also of the competence of his knowledge and influence – 'a family man who enjoys life, but whose pleasures are simple and unsophisticated'.

Another name which might crop up on the shortlist is that of the Queen of the Netherlands. Her connection with the British throne through the House of Orange is not as strong as that of certain other European monarchs, yet Queen Beatrix is of the right age, being nearly 60, and has the right experience to take on the job. She succeeded her mother Queen Juliana in 1980 when her mother abdicated, or 'retired'. A down side to her claim, not withstanding her remoter hereditary connection with the throne, is that her husband Prince Claus might be seen as too controversial a figure. He attracted flak from the Dutch public, many still with vivid memories of the Nazi occupation, having been born a German and lived during the Second World War on the German side.

One obstacle which might present itself in selecting a new monarch from an existing European royal family is the legal prohibition on any Roman Catholic sitting on the throne of the United Kingdom. This is not, as I suggested earlier, an insuperable problem. Given the constitutional upheavals which would be necessary to require the retirement of the House of Windsor, a change in the law of succession to remove the religious prohibition would be a relatively minor affair.

Given the Norwegian precedent at the beginning of the century, there is no reason why the parliamentary committee looking into the matter should not decide to approach the second or third child of a reigning monarch. They would be in a position to offer more of their time to the British job, as they would have no other obligations, while at the same time still being familiar with the duties of being a member of a royal house. They would also have been experienced in and possibly been hardened by the pressures that go with royalty in a modern age. Widening the net in that way there would be several dozen people to approach and discreetly sound out. The shortlist might also include members of the extended Windsor family – cousins whose less ostentatious ways might be well suited to a Scandinavian-style crown. Within the Scottish context, the option has been unofficially debated with the suggestion that the Princess Royal might ascend to the Scottish throne should Scotland become an independent nation.

So how might the selection of a new monarch take place in practice? Once the Government and members of the House of Commons felt that there was widespread political pressure to do something about the throne, replacing the Windsors with another family might well be the political compromise acceptable both to supporters of Queen Elizabeth II and the opposing republicans. Few people in Britain would stomach a republic with a president, certainly if he or she was a political figure, and supporters of the present monarchy, although they can find many arguments in favour of retaining a Crown, can find much to be said in favour of the present House of Windsor.

Let it be supposed then that after a major national debate (as outlined in the final chapter of this book), a committee is convened to draw up a list of possible successors to Queen Elizabeth II. At the same time, a date would have to be set for the Queen's handover and arrangements made for her future. There is no reason why the nation should not provide her with a house and a generous pension. If the Queen Mother is still alive, she could too be provided with a pension, although in all probability these constitutional changes would happen after her death. Indeed, they may even be prompted by her death. Once the period of mourning is over, it will be seen that the only representative of the days of the popular monarchy has passed.

In concluding his book, *Majesty: A Portrait of Elizabeth II and the House of Windsor*, Robert Lacey wrote of the Queen: 'She is a magical focus for affection pride and loyalty which the vast majority of her peoples are happy to accept.' Remember, this was being written at the time of the Silver Jubilee and much has changed since then. He then, significantly, went on to say:

> If they ever become unhappy with her or with the system that she represents, then she would have no doubt as to where her duty lay. 'We'll go quietly', is one of her favourite jokes.
>
> If Britain were one day to decide it no longer needed the monarch, then her response would be nothing but the logical continuation of her entire life. To comply, indeed, would be her ultimate service.

The Prime Minister of the day would go to the palace and talk the Queen through her options. She may well take the view that there is no point in selecting a date for her abdication until a successor is named. This point will be noted and indeed the work of the committee could be speeded up to enable a firm decision to be in place by the time of the proposed handover. All decisions, again as examined below, would need to be squared with the nation as a whole.

If it were decided to seek a new royal family, many discreet enquiries would need to be made by the committee of the potential candidates. Some, in loyalty, might feel that they cannot comply with any request unless they have Queen Elizabeth's approval. She is on close terms with most of the other European monarchs and is bound to take the view that if indeed her days are numbered, she would prefer someone known and trusted to carry on the traditions of monarchy than for the country to be plunged in to the unknown of republicanism. One can imagine many discreet phone calls being made between the Scandinavian royal palaces and those in Britain. The committee would also have to make other enquiries to make sure there were no scandals lurking in the other royal houses. Did the other houses have suitable heirs? Were they going through similar traumas to those of the House of Windsor? The Foreign Office would be involved.

What would be the political implications of forming new and very close alliances between Britain and one of her European partners? On this front there would probably be few problems as relations are at present, especially with those countries in the European Union, extremely close. Then, one day, at the final meeting of the committee, a name would be put forward to the Prime Minister. He or she would then ask the individual named whether, if invited, they would be prepared to carry out the duties of a constitutional monarch in the United Kingdom. The candidate chosen would at that stage no doubt want to enter a period of negotiation. What would be involved? What would be the time commitment? What would be the remuneration? What would be the constitutional implications for their own nation? Once satisfied and agreed, the Prime Minister could announce the name to Parliament. The next stage would be, subject to parliamentary approval, the holding of a referendum. The question would be simple. On such a date Elizabeth II would abdicate, her successor would be X, and the Windsor family would relinquish their claims to the British throne in order that (the named person) would be able to succeed. Does this have the approval of the nation, Yes or No?

At that stage, the contract between the proposed new Monarch and the nation would have to be hammered out. People would want to be satisfied that the new regime would be simple, cheaper and unostentatious and yet retain much of the dignity and tradition of the crown. The abdication deal with the Queen would need to be made public. Arrangements would have to be made to take over the royal palaces which the Queen would no longer need and which her successor would find surplus to requirements.

For the sake of argument, let us suppose that the Queen retires to a new home given to her by the nation. The new monarch would have a Scottish residence at the Palace of Holyroodhouse and a London residence, perhaps Kensington Palace or St James's, and all the other royal palaces would become museums. As

Hampton Court and the Tower of London do today, so Buckingham Palace, Balmoral, and Sandringham would echo to the sound of tourists' feet.

Assuming the British people accepted the proposal, the day of the handover would soon dawn. No doubt the Queen would be allowed to make a farewell address to the nation. Given her reputation for being able to suppress all her emotions beneath her solemn and rather hard exterior, she is unlikely to shed a tear on air. Privately, she may even breathe a sigh of relief that what had seemed to her a life sentence had been commuted. She could retire to the countryside and enjoy country life and raise horses without all the pressures that are on her, day in, day out, as Queen. For others in the family it would be a difficult move. No doubt the Prince of Wales would find suitable employment as figurehead for some environmental cause. Princess Margaret would retire as most other women of her age have done. Indeed all the members of the royal family might feel a sense of responsibility lifted from their shoulders. The spotlight of media interest would now be turned upon the new Monarch and the new royal house.

The role of the Princess of Wales can only be guessed at. As a charismatic figure she will undoubtedly continue to attract attention. She will however have to live off any means she might have negotiated following her divorce settlement. And how will the new retired Windsor family be addressed? No doubt, as happens with so many of the exiled royal families of Europe and other pretenders, the sycophantic clique around will pretend that all was normal. The Queen will be addressed as Ma'am or Your Majesty. Parliament might even allow her to retain a title of dignity, Queen Emeritus or the Duchess of Balmoral. She will, in any event, be the Duchess of Edinburgh. Other members of the royal family might be allowed to keep titles, but these titles will not be passed on. Alternatively, the Prince of Wales might just become Mr Charles Mountbatten Windsor, or as the son of a duke, Lord Mountbatten Windsor or Lord Merioneth if he is to take his father's second title, as is the custom with dukes and their heirs.

That day of handover would be one of mixed emotions for the people of Britain. Everyone would need to get used to a new name on the throne and a new head on the coins, as previous generations have done when Kings and Queens have died. Life would go on much as before. It will be a quiet day, rather like that following the natural death of a Monarch. There will be a certain relief too that at last a conclusion to an unhappy period has been reached.

By contrast, handing over to a president would be riotous and noisy. There would be much triumphalism. It would follow a long period of electioneering which would have opened up deep divisions in society. There would be a feeling amongst many people that they could not join in with the celebrations. They would feel a sense of loss. They would need to grieve at the departure of so much which was familiar, mourn for the destruction of so much of the country's heritage. This would not be through any love of the discredited Windsors but result from a pain at an attack on their very identity. Handing over the Crown to a new royal family would be a far less traumatic experience for everyone.

The scene as painted by Sue Townsend of the royal family being packed off to a council house is unrealistic. For there to be continuity of a civilized kind, the Queen would need to be allowed to retire with some grace and dignity. No doubt tabloids would attempt to get shots of furniture vans moving private possessions out of Buckingham Palace and heading up the motorway to the north of England, but much attention would be turned on the successor arriving in London for a simple but brief ceremony of proclamation.

It might well be decided, as a way of establishing the simpler style of monarchy, that a coronation be dispensed with. Drawing up a coronation service for the new Monarch would indeed be a nightmare for those involved. All the medieval baggage concerning the divine right of kings would have to be ditched, in place would be a simple oath or declaration of allegiance to the British people. This need not be performed in the context of a religious service at all, although the established Church would no doubt want a service later at which the new King or Queen was present. A simple declaration and taking of an oath standing before the throne in the House of Lords would perhaps be sufficient to mark the accession of the new Monarch. That evening, following the ceremony, the people of Britain could sigh a collective sigh of relief that the nightmare of the Windsor years was over.

# 8

## *A Crown Alternative*

Just before the start of every meeting of the General Assembly of the Church of Scotland, the Edinburgh traffic is momentarily halted to allow a sleek, black car to be driven with police escort from the royal Palace of Holyroodhouse to the Mound. Sharp-eyed observers will notice something special about the car, for as well as flying a Standard it has no registration number.

When it comes to a halt by the archway leading through the courtyard, past John Knox's statue to the steps up to the Assembly, the small group of onlookers, some perhaps expecting to see a member of the royal family, will be slightly surprised to see no recognizable public figure alighting, but a distinguished, although entirely unrecognized party.

It will be the party accompanying Her Majesty's High Commissioner arriving to take his – or very occasionally her – place at the Assembly, on a throne in the gallery overlooking the assembled ministers and elders of the Scottish Kirk.

Unrecognized he or she may be to the general public, but to members of the Assembly and to the entire Establishment of Scotland for the week's duration of the Assembly, Her Majesty's High Commissioner is the Monarch. He or she is given a police escort, can claim such perks as being able to drive in a car without registration plates, can fly the Queen's flags and entertain in her royal palace. Those who meet the High Commissioner are expected to address him or her as 'Your Grace', the Scottish equivalent of 'Your Majesty'.

Her Majesty's High Commissioner is appointed for every General Assembly and is normally selected from amongst the great and the good of Scotland. One year perhaps a judge; another, a member of a distinguished aristocratic family; only occasionally is Her Majesty's High Commissioner a well-known face – a retired politician, perhaps. 1996 is an exceptional year in that the Princess Royal will hold the post.

At the Assembly, the High Commissioner takes his or her place looking down on the Kirk's deliberations accompanied by the Purse Bearer, Chaplain and other members of the entourage. The position and ceremonial is a throw-back to the times when the General Assembly of the Church of Scotland was a troublesome body and the King or Queen needed to keep a close eye on it. With the King of Scotland from the time of James I onwards living much of his time south of the border, and communication between Edinburgh and London being slow and difficult, it was necessary for the Monarch to have a trusted viceroy in place.

As well as sitting in on deliberations and reporting back to the Queen, the High Commissioner enjoys a week living in the Palace of Holyroodhouse at the foot of Edinburgh's famous royal mile where he or she can hold court as a monarch. During that time, he or she will entertain royally, inviting a whole range of influential and interesting people to dine. Government ministers are frequent visitors as are foreign dignitaries. In addition the High Commissioner hosts a garden party and the Sovereign's Scottish bodyguard waits in attendance.

During the week, when not sitting in on debates the High Commissioner pays royal visits to schools and hospitals, receiving bouquets and curtseys as if a member of the royal family. Then, when the tenure of office is up, like Cinderella at midnight, all the trappings disappear and the High Commissioner goes back to his or her own home reduced to normal status.

For that short spell of office, the High Commissioner is the Sovereign. The position is similar to that of a Governor-General or Viceroy representing the Queen in her territories overseas, but arguably it is more than that. The High Commissioner is at the centre of the Scottish royal court which is, in effect, convened annally for those seven days

It is all an interesting tradition dating from a former age, but what relevance might it be to the future of the Windsors? Simply in that it suggests yet a further option which the British people might care to adopt following the abdication of the Queen. It is without doubt the cheapest option and perhaps is best described as the Crown Alternative.

Why have a president or a monarch or a new royal family, why not just a Crown? In the way that land can be Crown property and there can be Crown courts, the source of all power and authority in the nation could be deemed to be the Crown. It would not be an object or a person, but a notion. It would be an abstract ideal which could embody national identity and heritage and preserve the country, if desired, as a United Kingdom. Yet, at the same time, there would be no family or political interest so inextricably linked with the Crown that, should they fall from grace, the Crown itself would be tarnished.

There would, of course, be a need for a person to represent the Crown on occasions. When Heads of State of other nations visit, or when honours are to be bestowed, then a suitably dressed and articulate person is needed to perform certain tasks. This is where the Scottish model comes in. That person could be chosen from amongst the great and the good to serve as the Crown High Commissioner. He or she would not be in office for more than a year, and, as the Scottish system has shown, there is usually no problem in finding someone to serve in this capacity who has the maturity and personality to carry it off.

A great advantage of adopting this approach would be that there would be no need for a break with the country's heritage and traditions. The High Commissioner would open Parliament, attend the trooping of the colour, fly the standard at Buckingham Palace and invite people to garden parties.

In very rare circumstances, the High Commissioner might have to take political decisions, as a constitutional monarch might, but there would be advisers on hand and precedents to follow and this would only be a very small aspect of the role. Certainly, there is no reason to suppose that a High Commissioner would be any better or worse at performing a more delicate political task than an hereditary monarch.

How might the High Commissioner also preserve some of the religious mystique of the Crown? Certainly, if he or she continued to be the person who attended the General Assembly of the Church of Scotland and, south of the border, maintained a special link with the Church of England, an important element of national identity would be maintained. Yet it would seem improbable that the High Commissioner would ever be able to develop a charisma of his or her own to replace that which the Windsors have lost. Indeed, if he or she did develop a special rapport with the people, it could only be but an ephemeral reproduction of the original article, for the High Commissioner would have only a limited time in office.

What could happen however is that, borrowing the Prince of Wales's idea, the High Commissioner would be obliged to undertake, as part of an oath of office, to be the Defender of Faith. He or she need not be a member of an established, or even Christian church, but would have to be prepared to be the defender of religious freedom. It would be a public declaration that the nation is not simply a secular political body, but that its people aspire to something higher. As part of this undertaking, the High Commissioner could also help maintain the established churches as churches of the people and not the exclusive property of active members.

At present, Her Majesty's High Commissioner symbolizes the unique relationship which has developed between the established Church of Scotland and the Crown. The Kirk remains fiercely protective of its rights and independence and yet appears to cherish the special status and protection it enjoys by virtue of its close relationship with the Crown. When resident in Scotland, the monarch worships as a member of the Church of Scotland. Whenever the Queen is in residence at Balmoral, it is a familiar sight on Sunday mornings to see the royal party gathering at the local parish church. The Queen has her own chaplains in Scotland, normally a distinguished group of ex-moderators of the Church of Scotland and Scottish theologians.

One would suppose that, to be an active Presbyterian in Scotland and Supreme Governor of a catholic Episcopalian church in England, would require of the Queen a certain theological dexterity. The State Church of Scotland is Calvinistic in origin, evangelical in doctrine, and so Presbyterian in constitution that many of its members think and speak in the fiercest of hostile tones when it comes to anything to do with bishops. However, the Queen appears to have the ability to perform doctrinal somersaults, either that, or she has a total indifference to the niceties of inter-denominational debate. A Crown High Commissioner would need to adopt the same flexibility.

For the established churches, the Crown Alternative would have many advantages in maintaining their links with the past and with the people. For the abolition of the monarchy, or any major change to the present royal *status quo* which increased secularization, would inevitably impinge on the work of the churches. In theory, of the two established churches, the Church of Scotland would be least affected by an adoption of republicanism, as the Monarch, while currently deferred to and held in great affection, is nevertheless kept at a constitutional arm's length. However, the pageantry of the meeting of the General Assembly involves the Queen's deputy so completely that the whole tenor, status and standing of the event would be greatly diminished without a Monarch on the throne.

The Assembly is viewed by many in Scotland as a substitute parliament, indeed one of the most visible displays of Scottish separateness from England. Without the veneer of pomp which accompanies the Assembly, it would be reduced merely to being a business convention of worthy but dull, soberly dressed Presbyterians. Thus the continuing presence of a Crown High Commissioner visiting Edinburgh every May would ensure continuity.

The visible effect on the Church of England of the abolition or diminution of the monarchy would not be so immediately obvious. When the Church of England's General Synod meets, either in the circular chamber of Church House, Westminster or on the campus at York University, there is little or no pageantry. The formalities are conducted with barely any reference to the Queen. There is no grand throne in the gallery reserved for the monarch's representative. Even when the entire Synod gathers at York Minster for a choral Eucharist, it is but a drab affair when one has seen the Kirk at worship in Edinburgh's St Giles's Cathedral. For there, not only is Her Majesty's High Commissioner in prominence, but the entire court of Scotland. There is Lord Lyon with his heralds and pursuivants. There is the Queen's Scottish Household and her Royal Company of Archers. There are Knights of the Thistle and the holders of the hereditary offices are also entitled to attend. There is the hereditary Bearer of the Royal Banner of Scotland, even an hereditary Royal Carver. In the great procession will be seen judges in full wig and regalia, plus the dignitaries of the city and universities.

If the nation turned to republicanism, the Church of Scotland would be seen to suffer far more conspicuously than would its sister established church. Yet it would be the Church of England which would undergo the greatest constitutional and internal upheavals. The changes would be welcomed by many, but would be far-reaching and involve a wholesale revision of the appointment to bishoprics and other senior offices and, technically at least, a complete change in the status of the clergy. Presumably, too, it would be the end of certain curious ecclesiastical anomalies in which many Anglican historians delight. If there was no Queen, there would be no need for a Lord High Almoner to organize the distribution of the Queen's charitable gifts and to be responsible each year for the Royal Maundy service at which the Monarch distributes the specially minted silver Maundy money.

What too, under a republic, would become of the Deans of Peculiars? These are the historical leftovers of some 300 medieval office holders when the Monarch granted 'Peculiar' status, exempting an abbey, church or parish from episcopal control. The parish church of St Mary in Battle, East Sussex, for instance, does not have a vicar but a dean. And in Essex, at Bocking, since 1232 there has also been a dean; since 1572, the rector of Hadleigh in Suffolk has also had the title.

In another royal ecclesiastical anomaly, by tradition the National Anthem, when performed, must be sung to its own unique set of words. The Queen's Chapel of the Savoy is in the heart of London but exempt from any interference from the bishop of the diocese or even the Archbishop of Canterbury. She holds the Chapel as Duke of Lancaster, one of her many titles, and its curious status dates back to King Henry IV, who in 1399 annexed the Manor of the Savoy along with all the estates of the House of Lancaster. He declared them at the time to be a separate inheritance and consequently the words of the National Anthem are sung at every service in this form:

> *God save our Gracious Queen,*
> *Long live our Noble Duke,*
> *God Save the Queen.*

Under a president, all this, and indeed the more familiar National Anthem, would need to change.

The position of the Savoy Chapel and perhaps also other royal chapels in the absence of a Monarch would present lawyers with a fascinating and no doubt lucrative case. It might indeed be deemed that the Monarch holds rights separate from those of the Crown. Certainly, some of her homes, it can be argued, were bought as the personal property of the Windsor family and do not come with the Office of State. So a generous abdication or abolition contract might allow the Monarch to retain the Chapel of the Savoy, although it would probably mean she loses the right to appoint clergy to other royal Peculiars.

There is a strong case for saying that Windsor Castle is State, not Windsor family, property. Indeed, rights to personal ownership, it could be argued, were lost when a minister of the Crown took it upon himself after the fire, to declare that it would be the State and not the Queen who would pick up the bill for the uninsured damage. Consequently, the 'Queen's Free Chapel of St George within her Castle of Windsor' would become publicly owned. It is in this chapel, founded by Edward III, where the Knights of the Garter have their stalls. Today it is a self-governing community of priests and laymen, whose first duty is to celebrate divine service daily on behalf of the Sovereign and royal Household. Without a Sovereign to serve, it would make sense for the chapel to be taken over by the bishop of the diocese. Similarly, Westminster Abbey would become a national rather than royal church. And in all of these changes it would be a simple matter to substitute the notional Crown for the Sovereign, and have a High Commissioner carrying out the duties of the Queen.

Under a president, the question would remain as to whether these great and historic royal buildings with their strong religious connections, be in future viewed as the property of the secular state or whether they be handed over to the Church of England, which would inevitably in those republican circumstances become disestablished. Who has the greatest claim to these buildings, Church or State? For although Church and State today are seemingly intertwined, they are two very separate entities which could each make a claim for property in a republic. They might not appear to be separate entities, for it can be seen that the Prime Minister has certain powers of church appointment, and senior members of the Church sit in the House of Lords. The reality is, however, that the Prime Minister's advisory powers in church matters are solely exercised on behalf of the Monarch.

The Church of England is established alongside the secular government in that they both owe allegiance to the Sovereign. Parliament, which is the basis of secular government, has in almost all practical respects handed over its authorities to the synods and parliamentary structures of the Church. Even though the bishops still sit in one of the chambers of parliament, the House of Lords – the House of Commons, where secular power resides, makes no serious attempt any longer to interfere in church matters. Early this century this was not the case, when revisions to the Prayer Book were fiercely debated in the House of Commons. But today, although theoretically the House could have defeated the measure to allow the ordination of women to the priesthood, there was no serious likelihood of this happening. Following constitutional reform, the creation of the notional Crown could facilitate the untying of any legal tangles considerably.

From the Church's point of view, there is one main concern about the disestablishment which would result from wholesale changes to the British monarchy. That is that the Church would lose its position of being the Church of the nation, and that, as a result, the people of the nation would feel they no longer had a church to which they automatically belonged. While the trend in the Church of England today is towards the 'members only' approach, excluding from automatic church baptism or marriage those with no regular connection or commitment to the worshipping body, there are many who still feel that the Church must be open to all. In the past, because the Church was established, this commitment to the whole population by the Church did not need to be spelt out. The situation today is different, and a total disestablishment could well result in the dominance of the 'members only' approach.

Crucial to the maintenance of the Church as a national and open body is the maintenance of the parish structure. Both in Scotland and England, every church serves a defined geographical area, and there is no part of England or Scotland which is not contained within a parish. As long as this remains and individual churches do not become magnets to congregations seeking special types of worship, and the unchurched at large still feel an emotional commitment to the parish church, the idea can persist that the Churches of England and Scotland are there for all the people. The desirability of this is well expressed by a clergyman from Wiltshire who took part in a recent poll on the state of the Church of England. He said:

> I believe the Church of England must stand by the parish system, i.e. to have a personal relationship and commitment to all who reside in these islands who are not otherwise committed. We are not a sect or congregational set-up and must not...become one either.

A look at Wales confirms this more optimistic approach. While the Church in Wales is disestablished – and has been since the days of Lloyd George – it remains a national church because it has retained its parish structure. Whether it is a thriving church is, of course, a matter open to debate. There may well be pressure, following disestablishment, for the Church of England to seek to become a pro-active and not a re-active church. It will be argued that it is only the evangelically-minded, pro-active churches which are currently growing, and that the resources do not exist simply to maintain a parish structure for the benefit of non-churchgoers who might one day want to avail themselves of the Church's services.

In practical terms, a disestablished, 'members only' Church of England would deeply affect the general spiritual character of the nation. It may well become a more thriving body, but many people would feel excluded from it. People who felt that they could not sign up to a set of doctrines or commit themselves to the forms of worship now popular in most churches would increasingly find the Church of England an alien environment. The more exclusive the disestablished Church of England became, the fewer people would be welcomed by or feel comfortable in approaching the parish church for weddings, funerals or baptisms. There would thus be a growth in the secular forms, and bland crematorium funerals and Register Office weddings would predominate.

There is, then, an argument to be made for the Crown Alternative, in order to retain that special link between the established churches and the unchurched population at large. This argument is a strong one, especially if it is feared that the Church of England would become an increasingly exclusive sect as a consequence of the abolition of the Monarch. In defending faith, the High Commissioner would also defend the rights of every citizen to have access to the main national churches. The notional Crown, too, could be given responsibility for the care of buildings, parish churches and Peculiars alike. This would take from congregations the burden of maintenance and give the whole nation a greater sense of being part of the Church. Furthermore, the disestablished Church in Wales might wish to be returned to a status as a constitutionally recognized national church. By thus retaining an official constitutional recognition of the churches of the nation, it might help the moderating influences inside the churches wishing to curb or control the drive towards zealous exclusivity.

At one time, certainly in the late eighteenth and early nineteenth centuries, it could be said of the Church of England that it was the embodiment of the State in its religious aspect. In the words of Derek Jennings, in *A Church for the Nation*,

> Church and state were theoretically, and very largely in practice, two ways of expressing the reality of the English nation; one *vis-à-vis* the external world and the other in relation to God...the church had a certain autonomy but was expected to support the civil state and was in turn supported by it. The same interests bound both institutions and the monarch headed them both...there was felt to be

nothing in contemporary philosophical, political or scientific thought which forced a radical divergence of view between the secular and religious worlds...the state was articulating the needs of the Church and vice versa.

Today, things are very different, of course. At the time of which Derek Jennings was writing, there was no church parliament to focus any divergence even if there had been one between Church and State. Nowadays, the church parliament or Synod is a forum of debate which when political issues are at stake is, more often than not, a focus of criticism of the Government.

It can certainly not be said that the modern Church and modern British State share the same interests. But do they, nevertheless, remain as two ways of expressing the reality of the English nation? To unravel this question requires an examination of what is meant by the nation. The current debate about the future of the monarchy could be viewed as a symptom of a breakdown in national consensus. If the monarchy not only heads but epitomizes the nation, it follows that the monarchy is disposable if there is no longer a cohesive nation to represent. Britain has become multi-cultural in the obvious sense that there is now a substantial body of the population with cultural heritages very different from that of the people who would see themselves as indigenously British. But there are less obvious sub-cultures, and Britain has become far more fragmented. One pointer to this can be seen in the growth of choice in mass entertainment. At one time, it could almost be guaranteed that certain television programmes would be viewed by such a substantial number of people that they would be the talking point the next day. Currently, television and radio choice is so wide that many programmes survive and thrive as cult or minority interests.

More widely, the world is embarking on a debate about the future of the nation state. International communications and systems of finance have reduced national sovereignty substantially. Sub-national groups are re-establishing their identities throughout the world. The once all-powerful former Soviet Union is breaking up into its almost 'tribal' divisions, and even throughout the European Community regional identities are growing rapidly at the expense of the national.

In such circumstances it is not surprising that the old eighteenth- and nineteenth-century joint Church and State expression of the English nation no longer applies in anything like its old force. Perhaps it is therefore the case that, as there is no harking back to the old days, the removal of the Monarch and the consequent disestablishment of the churches would be an inevitable extension of an existing trend. Taking that view, it can be said that while the churches would alter in feel, style, status and duties in a Britain divested of its royalty, these changes would have happened anyway. As suggested above, the responsibility of the established churches to remain available to all the people would have to be addressed in any event, and a decision would have to be taken by the churches on whether to stay as part of the folk culture or become 'members only' denominations. The selection of the Crown Alternative model in preference to that of the republican model would at least ensure that the religious dimension to the constitutional and cultural debate was addressed.

# 9

## *The Will of the People*

No change to the British monarchy can today be contemplated without considering the Scottish and Northern Ireland dimensions. There is considerable pressure in Scotland for independence within the European Community. At the next General Election, it is very probable that the Scottish National Party will return sufficient members to parliament in Westminster that their cause cannot be ignored. Given that, in addition, both the Labour and Liberal Democrat parties want to see constitutional changes in Scotland, the United Kingdom as it is now formulated is unlikely to continue indefinitely.

Scotland and England were ruled over by two separate crowns until the accession of James VI of Scotland as James I of England. The two nations remained separate in most other ways until the Act of Union of 1707 was passed by both Houses of Parliament, the English and the Scottish. It was far from a universally popular move, and violent scenes occurred in various Scottish cities and anti-union protests were despatched from many of Scotland's burghs. The measure was described somewhat unflatteringly as 'a solid foundation for putting the two countries on one bottome [*sic*] to all posterity'.

In the event, the Act did not prescribe total uniformity in every respect, and even since becoming joint members of a United Kingdom, Scotland has continued with its separate legal system.

It also issues its own banknotes and maintains a separate royal Scottish court.

Many nationalists are also republicans. An independent Scotland they would hope would have an independent Scottish president. Nevertheless, as in England, there is a residual affection for the monarchy as an institution and certainly grave suspicion when it comes to the idea of a political president being in office. One solution might therefore be for the two crowns to be separated again and a separate King or Queen of Scotland be crowned. If this is not the will of the Scottish people, the Crown Alternative, based as the idea is on an existing Scottish practice, might be agreeable. But whatever course of action is decided upon, any change should ideally coincide with the proposed abdication of the House of Windsor as it would make for much constitutional convenience.

The difficulties arising in Northern Ireland are very different. For the Protestants there, republicanism is the enemy. They declare that they will not surrender to forces which would impose Catholicism or republicanism on them, and the two notions are perceived by many Protestant Unionists as interchangeable. Political discussion as to the future of Northern Ireland is fraught with difficulty. Much depends on maintaining the peace. It is a very fragile concept, as the events of February 1996 proved when the IRA cease-fire was shattered by the Docklands bomb in London which killed two people. In the Irish context, all political initiatives are hard to take.

The late Senator Gordon Wilson, a well-known peacemaker who sprang to fame when his daughter was killed by an IRA bomb in their home town, was always prepared to consider radical peace proposals without prejudging them and condemning them out of hand. One idea he once discussed involved a very radical approach. It was suggested as a long-term political solution that there be a united Ireland. However, this was not to be a republic to which Unionists, loyal to the Crown, would be obliged to give their unwilling consent. It was suggested that the new united Ireland explore a uniquely different solution, one which no nation state has ever before adopted. It was this: that people in the north and people in the south would be able to live and work side by side but opt to declare their loyalty to different institutions.

Those in the south might prefer to pledge their allegiance to a president, and those in the north to a crown. In a court of law, a defendant could choose to be prosecuted by the Crown or the State. Taxes could be paid to the Irish Republic or collected by a Crown inland revenue. There would be no duplication of services, all that would be required is for the citizen to choose one of two administrative packages. It would be no more disruptive of smooth government than a person in Wales opting to fill out a form in English rather than Welsh. The great advantage would be that no individual person's political or religious conscience need be violated.

It is, of course, not an immediate solution. However, in a generation or two, when the violence is hopefully long past, this might indeed become a viable approach. In the meantime, the Unionists of Northern Ireland wish to preserve the Protestant Crown of the United Kingdom. In practice, therefore, when the change-over is made, the new King or Queen or Crown of England would also need to become King or Queen or Crown of Northern Ireland. Any residual claims to being Monarch of the whole of the Republic as well would have to be dropped quietly. At the same time, under such a new regime, the flexibility would be there for further constitutional change should one of the radical proposals for political solution of the whole of Ireland be adopted.

Given the option of going in with the Republic or transferring loyalty to a new Monarch or Crown of England, the Unionists would undoubtedly choose the latter. Indeed, the symbolism in the province, especially at the time of the marching seasons, relies heavily not so much on Queen Elizabeth II but on monarchy and royalty generally. The banners and pictures to the fore show not the present monarch at all, but King William III, who, interestingly, was himself brought in from abroad to supersede a king who was forced off the thone. Given that history, and also the fact that many on the strictly moral religious right wing in Northern Ireland are strong upholders of family values, the decline of the House of Windsor and its replacement with an acceptable Protestant family from Europe or a notional Crown might indeed be welcomed.

The deposed king superseded by William of Orange and his wife Mary, was, of course, James II. Many nationalists in Scotland especially, remembering the 250th anniversary of the Battle of Culloden, will be well aware that it was this King's descendants who tried to reclaim the throne.

Most historians agree that following Bonnie Prince Charlie's landing in Scotland in 1745, and his capture of Edinburgh and initial victories, if he had only remained in Scotland and claimed the Crown of Scotland for himself, his campaign would have been an undoubted success. His mistake was to march south and then, swayed by his advisers, who had lost their nerve, to return to Scotland and not continue to London. This is what cost him the throne of Scotland and the entire campaign.

Bonnie Prince Charlie ended his days king in name only to his Jacobite followers. They drank the health of the king over the water, and he drank himself to death in Rome. His brother succeeded, but as a cardinal of the Church of Rome he was unmarried and had no heir, and to all intents and purposes the Jacobite claims fizzled out. It was all a sad and ignominious end to a gallant episode in history described by Bruce Lenman in his book, *The Jacobite Cause*, like this:

After 1754 Charles went into a definite physical and moral decline and his public reputation was ruined by reports of his excessive drinking. In 1760 his Scottish mistress Clementina Walkinshaw left him, taking with her their daughter Charlotte. Succession to his father's titles on the death of that tired old man in 1766, did not even stimulate Charles to issue the usual commemorative medallion, though his brother Henry, who had enraged Charles by accepting a cardinal's hat in 1747 had the Italian sculptor Fillipo Cropanese produce a commorative medallion of himself. The late 1760s saw Charles come under the sensible influence of a new secretary of state John Caryll, who negotiated his marriage with a minor German princess, Louisa of Stolberg-Gedern. The French, anxious for the procreation of a handy supply of Stuart pretenders, paid for the dowry, though their own last serious plan for an invasion of Britain on a Jacobite basis had foundered with the defeat of their Atlantic fleet in the battle of Quiberon Bay in 1759.

For a year or two Louisa was a political asset. Then the marriage began to sink. In 1775 Charles sacked Caryll. In 1780 a more than usually violent St Andrew's Day binge by Charles made his wife leave her alcoholic spouse, first for a convent, then for her lover Alfieri. Formal separation was acknowledged in 1784, when Charles re-activated his relationship with his daughter Charlotte, whom he legitimated as Duchess of Albany. She nursed him through to death in January 1788.

Jacobitism as a cause was dead. Even the non-juring Scots Episcopalians agreed to pray for George III after 1788. By then the Jacobite aristocracy of the Highlands had engineered its reconciliation with the Hanoverian regime, mainly by raising regiments for overseas service for the British army.

However, the cause had not entirely fizzled out and there are many still living who maintain the Jacobite claim to the throne is the legitimate one.

Today, the Duke of Bavaria is the representative and 'heir general of King Charles I', or, as the Stuarts describe him, 'senior descendant of James VI of Scotland, James I of England and lineal heir of the royal House of Stuart'. He is therefore the Stuart claimant to the British throne, but as he leaves any pretence in abeyance he has been seen as no threat to the British Monarch. Yet it is interesting to note rumours that his grandson, who may one day inherit the claim and the title, was born in Britain and his birth attended to or attested to by two peers as Members of Parliament. The Jacobite claim might be dormant but it is not dead. An option for Scotland may well be to invite a descendant of the House of Stuart to be a new separate Scottish monarch.

Of course, the present House of Windsor has a lineal descent back to the Stuarts and, in nationalist circles, the name of the Princess Royal has been suggested unofficially as a possible new Queen of Scotland to establish a new royal line. How she would react to a formal proposition is of course open to question. She would no doubt feel a great deal of loyalty to the House of Windsor, but if it were the will of the people and the will of Parliament she might feel it her duty to accept. One proviso might be, laid down by both Princess Anne and the Scottish people, that her successor should not necessarily be her first born but a suitable family member with the right hereditary connections who was up to the job and prepared to take on the responsibilities. Indications are that the House of Windsor is currently preparing for this scenario as a back-up survival plan. The 1996 Queen's High Commissioner to the General Assembly of the Church of Scotland was significantly and uniquely a monarch's daughter – Princess Anne. She has of late been strengthening her ties with Scotland opting to be married by the Presbyterian church. Even her son has chosen to play rugby for Scotland.

Despite republican sentiments within the party, official Scottish National Party policy is to continue with the Queen as Head of State, as a constitutional monarch whose duties are set out within a written constitution, with the Chancellor of Scotland (the Speaker of the Scottish Parliament) acting as Head of State when the Queen is absent from Scotland. Alex Salmond MP, who speaks for the party on constitutional matters, believes it might be somewhat premature and fanciful to contemplate Princess

Anne setting up a junior Windsor dynasty in Scotland. He has, however, noticed how 'she has been assiduously promoted as the Scottish member of the royal family since the Queen Mother has been obliged through old age to become less active'.

No doubt if Scotland was to have a monarch of its own for the first time for almost 400 years, it would want to revive some of the traditions of the Monarch. Yet at the same time, true to the modern age, it would no doubt be felt by the nationalists that too much ostentation was inappropriate. A simple Presbyterian blessing and declaration in St Giles's Cathedral appropriate to the modern age would suffice, and the Monarch could then live in a modest manner in an apartment at the Palace of Holyroodhouse. He or she would open the new Scottish parliament, and carry out other duties as might be required of a constitutional monarch. Balmoral could serve perhaps as a secondary residence and would be a fine place to entertain foreign dignitaries or hold government conferences when ministers needed to get away from the capital.

There are clearly a number of options open to the British people. There is no single alternative to the Queen, that being the unattractive possibility of a republic and political president. The House of Windsor could reform from the inside. The first priority would be to require the present Queen to retire. Then Prince Charles could be bypassed in favour of one of his siblings or a cousin. Prince William might inherit from his grandmother with Princess Diana standing in as Queen Regent.

If it were felt, however that the House of Windsor was incapable of internal reform and could never recreate its mystical inheritance, the entire family could be obliged by the people to step aside and a new family take their place. Taking the possibilities of reform further, the Windsors could be replaced by a notional Crown, an idea which might prove attractive to the Scots and the people of Northern Ireland. There will no doubt be other ideas which will emerge as the debate grows. What needs to be recognized is that, should it be felt the monarchy as now arranged has failed, it is safe to declare the fact and start the search for the acceptable alternative.

So how might it come about that the House of Windsor be replaced by any of the options outlined above?

First of all, the Government of the day would have to discern a demand from the British people for change. Already, Tony Blair has introduced the very limited idea of a constitutional change involving the abolition of the hereditary peers' rights to vote in Parliament. In doing this, Tony Blair has placed the subject of wider reform on the agenda. Although most observers believe voters are more interested in economics, it could be possible that constitutional reform will become a debating point at the General Election, with the Conservatives arguing to preserve the Union in the face of all the opposition parties wanting some degree of greater Scottish self-determination. With the search for a lasting peace in Northern Ireland still very much to the fore, the debate could be widened to include long-term political solutions to the Irish troubles. The Liberal Democrats will be pushing for proportional representation and a Bill of Rights. More important, however, in getting constitutional changes onto the electoral agenda would be if the election came at a time of great upheaval, disgrace or conflict within the royal family. In those circumstances, the future of the monarchy would inevitably become an electoral issue.

Once the mood for change existed, the matter would need to be formally tested. One way of doing this would be through a referendum, asking the electorate if it be the will of the people that the House of Windsor be removed. A possible question for the ballot paper might be: 'Should a committee of Parliament be instructed to explore options whereby the House of Windsor can be replaced?'

A majority vote in favour would enable Parliament to set the ball rolling. One possible timetable of events might be that Queen Elizabeth II would abdicate and retire at the end of the millennium, midnight 31 December AD 2000, allowing the dawn of 1 January 2001 to welcome in the reformed Constitution.

Prior to that date, a second referendum would need to be held, setting out Parliament's preferred alternative to the Windsors. This would have been arrived at after the widest possible sounding of opinion in the nation.

Let us suppose the solution offered was that of republicanism. That would be voted on. If it failed to achieve a majority popular vote, a second option would be offered. This time there might be general support for inviting a member of a European royal family to form a royal house. At that point the decision would be taken, the Queen informed and she would, in all probability, go quietly.

Another way of running the referendum could be to set out three or four options and ask people to indicate their preferences and then, using an agreed counting method, the will of the people could be understood.

The weakness of the Tony Benn Bill was that it both removed all mystery from the constitution and that it tackled too many socialist ideas at the same time. Its strength was that it did suggest that the opportunity offered by a reform of the Crown should not be lost and that other constitutional changes should be initiated simultaneously.

So, a programme of limited parallel change could be contemplated. This might include Scottish self-government, parliamentary reform (including an overhaul of the voting system), the introduction of basic rights enshrined in law, and the associated removal of the legal assumption that British people are subjects and not citizens.

To be a subject is to be living in, or under, a system of government which is still rooted in the feudal. To be a subject is to be under the subjection of the Monarch, to owe obedience without personal independence or freedom. Of course, in practice, British people enjoy a large degree of freedom, but, when the Government or the courts or the police wish to have their own way, there is little the subjected citizen can do. Indeed, in a recent legal ruling it was argued that in law every child is the property of the Queen.

However, before any move is made to remove the House of Windsor, it must be accepted by the nation that this can be done. Certainly, if it is the Will of the People, there can be no impediment. But what if monarchists argue that to remove the Queen would be an ecclesiastical impossibility? There are those traditionalists who hold, almost as an article of religious faith, that once a Monarch has taken his or her solemn vows at the coronation, the bond between Monarch and nation is one for life.

Here, the traditionalists need to reread the Old Testament where they will find the original references to the most solemn and deeply spiritual coronation ritual of all, that of the anointing. Going back to the roots of this symbol of divine grace, it will be seen that when Solomon was anointed king by the prophet, it was on the instructions of the ruling King of Israel, who was in effect abdicating. He was on his deathbed and acutely aware of the political urgency of handing over to a new ruler and so selected Solomon, who was not – and this is also a relevant point for supporters of the House of Windsor to note – his first-born son. Indeed, he was not in line to succeed and yet was chosen by David and, through anointing, approved by God, to be the new king. If the sacred undertakings of Queen Elizabeth at her coronation are to be used as an argument against her abdicating and handing over to a new Royal House, then the sacred imagery of the coronation can equally be used to justify an abdication and the enthronement of someone other than the Queen's first-born son.

And what would the ex-Queen Elizabeth do? There can be no objection to her being allowed to retire on a generous pension. Even Tony Benn allowed for this. She could live out her days following country pursuits with her immediate family around her if she wished. And where would she live? It is said that she and Prince Philip already have their eye on a valley in Lancashire in the beautiful Forest of Bowland which would make an ideal retirement home.

# By Sex Divided

*The Church of England and Women Priests*

Jonathan Petre

By the summer of 1994, more than 1200 women had been ordained as priests in the Church of England, bringing to an end one of the most turbulent chapters in recent ecclesiastical history. Few issues have provoked such rancour and bitterness, division and dissent. *By Sex Divided* captures some of the flavour of these extraordinary times – from the early struggles of women to make their voices heard to the dramatic *dénouement* on 11 November 1993, and its aftermath.

Jonathan Petre, a journalist who covered much of the debate, calls on the observations of some of the leading protagonists including Dr Robert Runcie, his successor as Archbishop of Canterbury Dr George Carey, Dr Graham Leonard, Peter Geldard, George Austin, Diana McClatchey and Joyce Bennett.

The Archbishop of Canterbury, Dr George Carey, is now involved in a damage-limitation exercise attempting to reconcile the opposing views and to accommodate those who feel uneasy about women priests within the Church. Petre examines the effects of this issue and the future now facing the Church of England.

'If anyone wants to know how it really felt to be there, and how the Church arrived at where it is now, the most graphic and accurate account so far is in *By Sex Divided*...'
*Church Times*

# The Soul of Politics

## A Practical and Prophetic Vision for Change

### Jim Wallis

With his first book in several years, Jim Wallis reinforces his reputation as one of the most powerful Christian voices of the modern era, a voice raised once more against the oppression of the weak by the powerful.

*The Soul of Politics* responds specifically to the signs of cultural breakdown and political impasse in Western societies: the absence of community, the widespread poverty, the violence, racism and sexism.

The book is a marvellous balance of sophisticated analysis and fascinating stories, as Wallis tours the world looking for 'signs of transformation'. From the gangs of Los Angeles to the peasants of the Philippines, and in the revolution that transformed South Africa, something dramatic is underway.

As the acquisitive eighties are left behind and we bask in the idea of the more 'caring' nineties, Jim Wallis's book is both a sharp reminder of cold reality and an encouraging manifesto for change.

'What a thrilling, exhilarating experience reading *The Soul of Politics*. It is riveting stuff, just what the doctor ordered for a hardened, cynical and disheartened and disillusioned world... This book shows how it is possible for all of us to become more human, living in an environment that is hospitable to people, where they matter, where justice and compassion and caring are at a premium. A tremendous and timely book.'
*Archbishop Desmond Tutu*

# A Celtic Resurrection

## The Diary of a Split from the Church

### Robert Van de Weyer

The 'defrocking' of Norfolk priest Kit Chalcraft in 1995 for seeking to marry for the third time has put the Church of England's moral respectability firmly in the spotlight. But, when Chalcraft's parishioners refused to accept the appointment of a new vicar by the local bishop of Norwich, the affair sparked wider questions about who decides who are to be the ministers of the people.

Cambridgeshire pastor Robert Van de Weyer answered a plea from Chalcraft's congregation to minister to them, despite instructions from his own bishop in Ely not to cross diocesan boundaries. In this personal and challenging diary, he charts the tensions, hopes and fears of a people who feel let down by an institution which they claim has squandered its resources and failed to provide adequate leadership.

He argues that, far from being isolated incidents of rebellion, the unfolding stories represent a positive return to a Celtic model of Christianity in Britain. Drawing on strands throughout history – from Ss Cuthbert and Aidan to modern-day Sudan – Van de Weyer explores this model, where people manage their own pastoral affairs. One where priests and bishops, unburdened from centralized bureaucracy, become travelling preachers, bringing their spiritual wisdom from church to church.

# *Agenda for the Third Millennium*

His Holiness Pope John Paul II
Translated by Alan Neame

No one is more concerned about the progress of the human race as it enters the third millennium than the Pope himself, John Paul II. He predicts a time in which there may be a great reawakening to the Gospel of Christ. On the other hand, he documents the ever-increasing threats to human life.

Collecting his writings and speeches – published and unpublished – under ten major headings, *Agenda for the Third Millennium* shows once again the Pope's extensive knowledge of world affairs and acute understanding of the human condition.

In what amounts to a sequel to his bestselling *Crossing the Threshold of Hope*, John Paul II addresses Faith, the Church, Prayer, Love, History, Evil, Work, the World, Peace and Religion. Among the many controversial subjects discussed therein are the position of the laity in the Church, contraception and population control, feminism, money, unemployment, human rights, the ecological movement and Islam.

# *Like Water in a Dry Land*

## *A Journey into Modern Israel*

### Bettina Selby

In December 1994, at a time of intense political initiative for peace in the Middle East, Bettina Selby set off on a journey from Cyprus to the Holy Land. Riding her bicycle wherever possible, she travelled through Lebanon, Syria and Jordan to Jerusalem. Her final destination was a city she knew and loved, so much so that the political turmoil of recent years had made her unwilling to return.

Now, spurred on by the Jordan/Israel peace treaty and an audience with King Hussein, Bettina felt that at last perhaps a new perspective on Israel could be achieved. Over the next two months, she travelled widely, from the ruins of Byblos in Lebanon to the Armenian Cathedral Church in Jerusalem, to the refugee camps of Gaza. In every place she was offered the hand of friendship by people of diverse race and culture.

What begins as an enjoyable and quirky travelogue fast becomes a compelling critique of Middle Eastern politics, and its historical and religious foundations. In clear and lyrical prose, Bettina Selby has produced a fascinating account of her travels and a valuable contribution to our understanding of the modern Holy Land.

Bettina Selby is one of Britain's best-loved travel writers, with a string of books to her credit. Her mode of transport is usually bicycle. Her books include *Riding to Jerusalem*, *The Fragile Islands*, *Riding North One Summer*, *Riding the Desert Trail*, *Beyond Ararat*, and, most recently, *Pilgrim's Road: A Journey to Santiago de Compostela*.